ORIGAMI
MADE EASY

Kunihiko Kasahara

D0110921

JAPAN PUBLICATIONS, INC.

© 1973 by Kunihiko Kasahara

First edition: September 1973
Twenty-second printing: September 1992

LCC Card Number 73–83956
ISBN 0–87040–253–6

Published by
JAPAN PUBLICATIONS, INC., TOKYO AND NEW YORK

Distributors:
UNITED STATES: *Kodansha America, Inc., through Farrar, Straus &
Giroux, 19 Union Square West, New York, 10003.* CANADA: *Fitzhenry
& Whiteside Ltd., 91 Granton Drive, Richmond Hill, Ontario, L4B 2N5.*
BRITISH ISLES AND EUROPEAN CONTINENT: *Premier Book Marketing
Ltd., 1 Gower Street, London WC1E 6HA.* AUSTRALIA AND NEW
ZEALAND: *Bookwise International, 54 Crittenden Road, Findon, South
Australia 5023.* THE FAR EAST AND JAPAN: *Japan Publications
Trading Co., Ltd., 1–2–1, Sarugaku-cho, Chiyoda-ku, Tokyo 101.*

Printed in U.S.A.

Preface

In good origami, the folding process itself is as important as the finished work. If the folding has been laborious, excessively complicated, and wasteful, all these faults will manifest themselves in origami that is stiff, unattractive, and messy. But, if the folding is economical and rational, the finished origami is certain to please. The economy and efficiency of the folding method become the characteristic traits of the folded figure and, in this way, give direct expression to the simple, but expressive, qualities of paper.

To carry this line of thought slightly farther, I can say that, in devising new origami that can be folded with ease and economy, a rational design route is essential. That is to say, using just any old folding method in any number of haphazard combinations will never give effective, attractive representation to the form you are attempting to create.

The aim of this book is to enable you to take full advantage of the pleasure to be had from making beautiful origami. One aspect of this pleasure is the fact that you can fold paper figures anywhere and at any time. The works shown in this book require no special equipment, scissors, or glue. I hope that when you go on a trip or when you have a few minutes of spare time while you are waiting for someone or something, you will slip this book and a few pieces of square paper in your pocket and use your leisure time to enjoy making origami. The first chapter is devoted to presenting a clear method for creating your own origami without time-consuming effort. The book is small, but I have tried to fill its pages with a maximum amount of helpful information.

July 4, 1973

Kunihiko Kasahara

Contents

Symbols and Folding Techniques

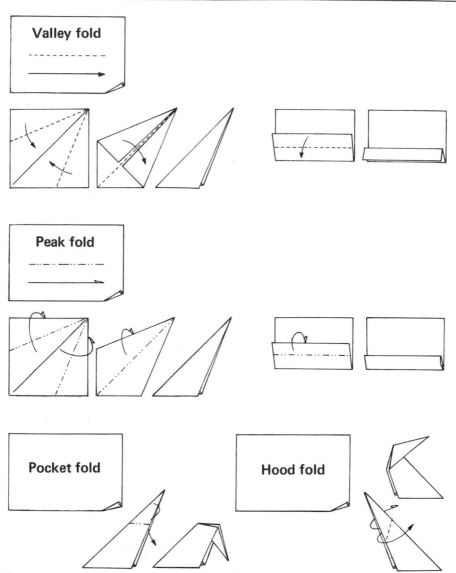

Valley fold

Peak fold

Pocket fold

Hood fold

1

Fundamentals

In using the word *fundamentals* I do not intend to give the impression that origami folding requires a great deal of complicated basic knowledge. In fact, the fundamentals of origami can be boiled down to two items. First, in order to enjoy making the origami figures in this book, you will need to understand the conventionalized symbols used in the charts and you must be able to perform a few basic techniques. The minimum of what might be called the rules of the origami game are found on p.6. If you wish to do no more than reproduce the origami shown in this book, you need only memorize these basic techniques and symbols and skip to Chapter Two, where you can immediately begin folding.

But the basic purpose of this book is to help as many people as possible learn to create new origami of their own. Teaching originality, the greatest happiness to be had from origami, is my constant aim. Consequently, I offer the following section as an introduction to the way in which you can produce your own origami. The principle on which the method is based is extremely simple, but the pleasure to be had from origami differs greatly depending on whether or not you know this system. If you will read it with an open mind and with the desire to learn what it has to offer, I am certain that you will find that it greatly stimulates and encourages your own creative will and abilities.

1. Turn the figure over
2. Open the figure out flat
3. Cut off
4. Stairstep fold
5. Part now concealed or the former position of a part
6. Indication of special steps, indications to pull a part out, or to inflate a part, or the order in which folds are made

Before beginning the route to origami originality, I must explain the symbols used to indicate folding methods. As I have already said, the symbols on p.6 are sufficient to the needs of the origami game, but a few additional ones are required for the works shown in Chapter Two and the rest of the book. The accompanying chart shows the most important ones, which are easily understood at a glance. Since these symbols are self-apparent, there is no need to memorize them: their meanings will be perfectly clear in all cases. Unlike architectural plans or mechanical designs, origami explanatory charts are approximate in nature. Always keep in mind the fact that natural folding methods are the basis of all the explanatory symbols. For convenience, the names of the symbols and the processes they describe are listed above.

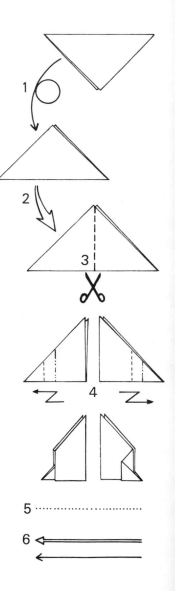

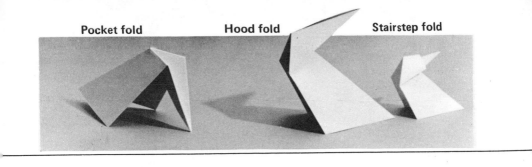

Pocket fold　　　　　　Hood fold　　　　　　Stairstep fold

First Step Toward Originality

Folding method is much more important than symbols. Whereas symbols are no more than a means employed in books for transmitting certain examples of origami, folding method is an integral part of the composition of all origami. The photograph above shows no more than a few basic folding methods, but the resulting folds already give a sense of lively expressiveness. For instance, the fold on the left is well known to Japanese children as a crow. In fact, it looks like that bird pecking at a bit of food. Sometimes children play with this fold by tapping one corner and making the figure jump forward.

But this is a special case. Generally, folding techniques are means to achieve given forms. Obviously, it is easier to produce the desired effect or create the desired form if you know more than one technique to use in striving to achieve your end.

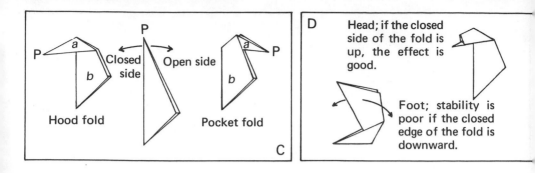

Hood fold: P a, Closed side, Open side, P a, b; Pocket fold — C

D Head; if the closed side of the fold is up, the effect is good.

Foot; stability is poor if the closed edge of the fold is downward.

Hood fold

This fold and the following pocket fold are essential to a knowledge of origami, no matter whether you wish to copy standard forms or create your own new ones.

To make the hood fold, it is possible to make the peak and valley folds in the order shown in Chart *A* and then simply pull the point in step *3* upward as indicated by the arrow. It often happens, however, that in the process of making an origami figure, this method produces too many unwanted creases and is consequently difficult to execute. For that reason, it is a good idea to practice making the hood fold in one step. This is easy to do, if, as shown in step *2* of *B*, you make a firm crease in the paper after determining the angle at which you want to make the fold.

The difference between the hood fold and the pocket fold depends on whether the open side or the closed side of the fold is upward. Interestingly enough, after folding, the distinction between the two folds ceases to exist in that if part *a* in Chart *C* is a hood fold, part *b* naturally becomes a pocket fold. You will find memorizing the forms in chart *D* helpful in producing good forms in creative origami.

1

2

3 Pull ou[t]

4

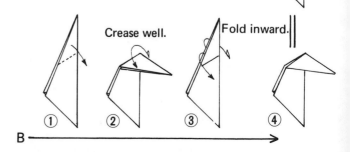

Crease well.   Fold inward.

① ② ③ ④

B ⟶

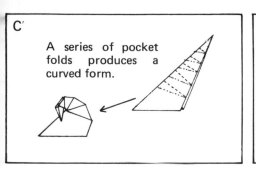

C′

A series of pocket folds produces a curved form.

D′ 1   2   3

Because in both 2 and 3, the open edge of the fold is turned downward, the forms have great stability.

Pocket Fold

Since this is only the hood fold turned inside out, it is possible to follow the order shown in A′ to make the pocket fold. But once again the use of valley folds makes the process more difficult. The pocket fold is actually very easy, however; and if you determine the angle as in B′, it can easily be produced in one step.

Characteristically the pocket fold is especially interesting in series. It can be used to produce the kind of curve shown in C′. Though this looks difficult, it is in fact quite simple, as you will learn if you fold it once. The pocket fold is frequently used to make the feet of birds and other animals (D′). When the point must face the rear, one fold is sufficient (D′-2), although two are required if the point must face forward (D′-3). The pocket fold provides greater stability because its open edge is downward.

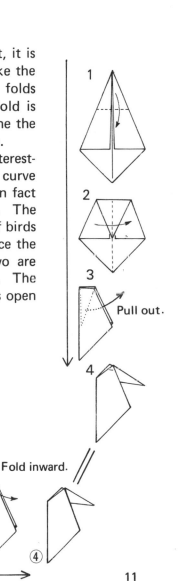

1

2

3

Pull out.

4

Crease well.   Fold inward.

① ② ③ ④

B′ ⟶

Other Techniques

The techniques shown here are important, but they do not cover all of the folding methods used in origami. For instance, there are methods used to produce solid forms, like the boxes in the photograph on p.13, and others needed for the open shapes of flowers like that in photograph on the next page. But the important thing at this stage of origami learning is to master a few methods instead of trying to become superficially acquainted with a large number.

Stairstep Fold: As the name indicates, this step fold is made by combining a valley and a peak fold to form a kind of pleat. Made in a series, the stairstep fold produces the lovely accordion-pleats fold seen in the shell on p.15. Made on slanting lines, the stairstep fold becomes something similar to the pocket fold (*B*).

Pull Fold: This fold, used to make the tip part of an angle slender, is often found in tails of origami animals or in the heads of origami human figures. In some cases, the paper is pulled forward as in *A* and *B*; in others the paper is tucked inward. In either case, the fold is easier to make if proper creases are made beforehand. For reference see the tropical fish on p.94.

Pinch Fold: Like the pull fold, the pinch fold is used to narrow part of a corner, though in the latter there is no pleat or step as there is in the former. The fold is complete at step *2*; depending on the nature of the paper, this fold can produce great stability (see penguin on p.57). The narrow tip can, however, be folded further to produce the shape in step *3*

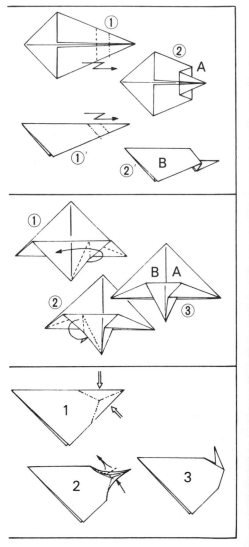

Curling: As a finishing touch for flower petals, animal tails, or moustaches, curling is most effective.

Inserting: For good examples of the effectiveness of this technique, see the mask on p.111 and the bottom of the sailboat on p.29.

Twisting: This is especially good for use with' foll papers, see the candle on p.38 and the jingle bells, on p.41.

Pulling: Interesting effects result from pulling series of stairstep folds.

Squashing: This technique is widely used. If side *a* of step *3* were to be turned to the left, the effect would be that of a pocket fold.

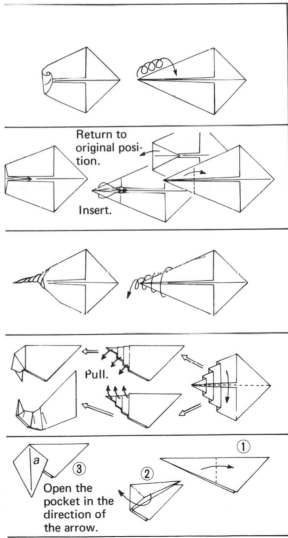

Return to original position.

Insert.

Pull.

Open the pocket in the direction of the arrow.

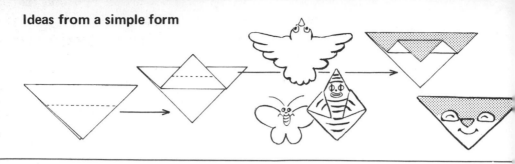

The Power of Association

Let us take a plain square piece of paper and fold it diagonally. Quite naturally, the result is a triangle, but we must not underrate this particular triangle. If we had cut the paper, the triangle would have been more or less limited to its own shape; but since we have produced it by folding, it has much greater meaning. The following are some of the characteristics of this folded triangle.

1. If we open it slightly, it will stand on its own.
2. The hypotenuse consists of two layers of paper.
3. The triangle contains space within the two layers of paper.

All of this is obvious; but if we let our imaginations take wing and apply the powers of association to this simple figure, a number of interesting things can be shown.

If I may be permitted a personal reference, I should like to call your attention to the origami work in the photograph at the bottom of this page. I am especially proud of it because my three-year-old son made it while I was working on the manuscript for this book. Of course, it was accidental; my child was only playing with some paper. After bringing me a number of unidentifiable objects that he had made and asking me what each one was, he showed me this. I immediately saw that the two layers of the folded right angle had been cleverly used to form a mouth. I praise this not because my son produced it, but because it is a very good origami idea. I believe that my son did know that it was a mouth because he told me the fold was frog.

But even setting my parental pride aside, I can say that this incident taught me much about the powers of association. The photograph at the top of the page illustrates how many things associative thinking can find in a square piece of paper folded into a triangle and then folded again so that the point of the upper layer is turned to the top.

Examine the folds made from a single sheet of square paper and shown on p.15. These are simple folds requiring no special creativity or skill; but if you apply your imagination, you will be able to see in them many different things. I find *4a* especially interesting because, although its outline is triangular, it acutally has four points. To test your associative abilities, see if you can tell which of the forms in the chart is the basis of the seashells in the photograph at the top of the page.

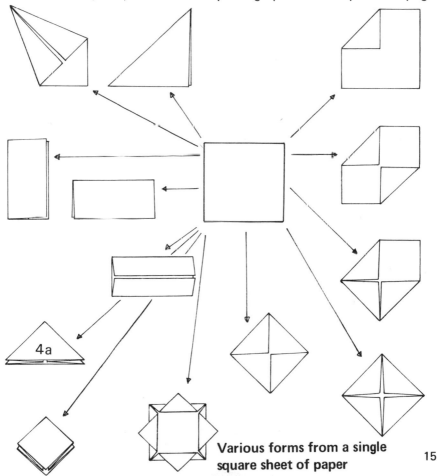

4a

Various forms from a single square sheet of paper

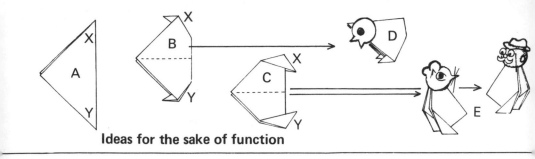

Ideas for the sake of function

To examine further the possibilities of association that can result from simple folding, please look at the chart at the top of the page. Corners *X* and *Y* of triangular fold *A* have been given pocket folds to form *B* and hood folds to form *C*. The resultant figures were then folded in half on the dotted lines to form *D* and *E*. By adjusting the angles of the hood or pocket folds, it is possible to make the figures stand on their own. You can see, then, that these figures come to life. It is true that they do not represent any particular object, but they are filled with all kinds of fresh associative possibilities. First, on the functional level, these figures are actual experiments with the idea that hood and pocket folds enable origami figures to stand. As the middle chart on p.17 shows, it is possible to expand the functional possibilities of simple origami to create figures that move. Or, as the lower chart shows, effective use can be made of the space enclosed by a simple fold to produce a container. In short, there are almost no limits to the possibilities inherent in origami, if you will use your powers of association.

I hope that what I have said so far has aroused your interest and strengthened your self-confidence in creative origami. But to go one step further, please look at the drawings at the top of p.17. These simple figures show how the positioning of a fold and the viewpoint from which it is seen can alter its image. Of course, I do not insist that you must try to make a single fold become a girl, a dog, or a cat. I am merely saying that instead of looking at a form from one point or in one position, you will discover much richer possibilities if you will turn it in many different ways and examine it from several angles. Always use origami techniques as ways to stimulate and make good application of your associative powers.

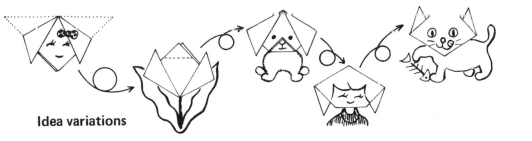

Idea variations

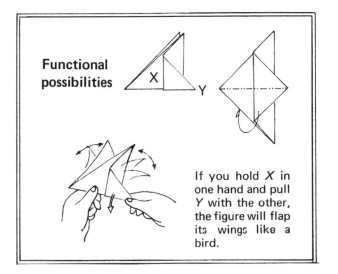

Functional possibilities

If you hold X in one hand and pull Y with the other, the figure will flap its wings like a bird.

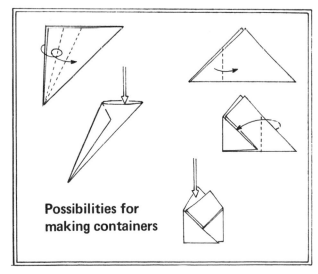

Possibilities for making containers

Compound Origami

Now that you have seen the possibilities of simple folding, I should like to introduce the idea of compound origami. In the preface to this book, I said that good and truly beautiful origami require that there be no waste and no excess completion in the folding process. Compound origami is an excellent way to achieve this end under certain circumstances. For instance, when the object or animal you want to represent is complicated, it may be possible to produce it with only one sheet of paper; but the end results of your labor are certain to look strained and to involve a great deal of waste in both time and material. There are some specialists who treat origami as if it were some kind of magic. They insist that all figures must be made of one, and only one, sheet of paper. Their approach may make origami a fascinating puzzlelike game, but it is by no means guaranteed to produce beautiful results. If loveliness is your aim, I strongly recommend that you divide the object you are trying to create into top and bottom, front and back, or right and left halves. You may then fold each half separately and join them in a compound origami that will be closer to your mental image and more attractive in appearance than the figure you would have produced if you had struggled to make it of one sheet.

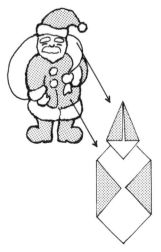

The illustration at the top of the page gives some examples that are simple, but I think you will agree imaginative, ways in which this can be done. The Santa Claus at the bottom of the page employs the interest of two-color paper.

On the preceding page I have shown how association gives birth to many interesting forms from a single piece of folded paper.

18

But as you use your imagination to devise more images, you will find that the things you want to make become increasingly complicated and difficult to execute. Compound origami enables you to express surprisingly wild flights of fancy simply and effectively.

The head is made from a piece of paper one-quarter the size of the piece used for the body.

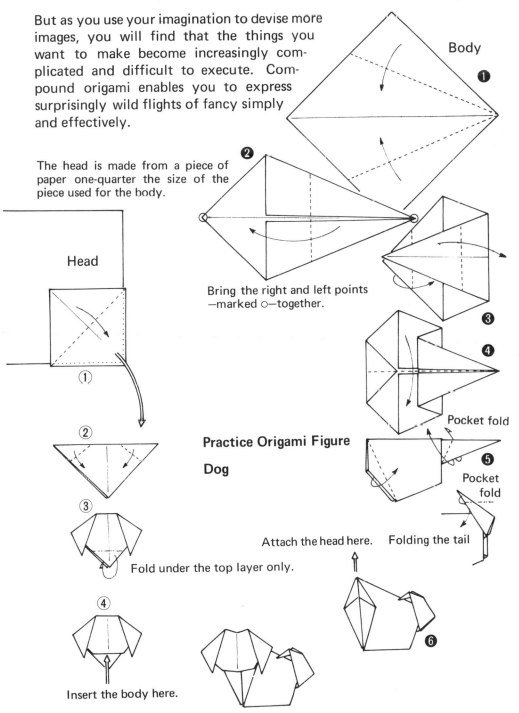

Body

❶

❷

Bring the right and left points
—marked ○—together.

❸

❹

Pocket fold

❺

Pocket fold

Head

①

②

③

Fold under the top layer only.

④

Insert the body here.

Practice Origami Figure

Dog

Attach the head here.　　Folding the tail

❻

19

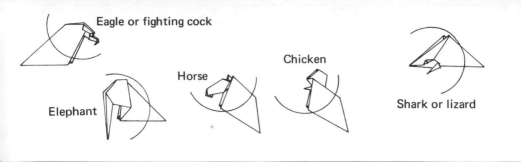

From Devising Parts to Total Expression

Before rounding out my remarks on the route to follow in devising your own original origami, I must say a word or two about self-confidence. When you have started creating your own folds, you will discover the inexhaustible pleasure of this creative act. But at first you might think that invention of this kind is beyond your powers. You must, however, rid yourself of such preconceived ideas and develop confidence in your own abilities. Perhaps you have already made the cat and Santa Claus that I recommended, and maybe the finished products are not as beautiful as you want them to be—even if a third party is able to identify what you were trying to make. But do not be overly concerned about the quality of your first attempts. The important thing is that you now have in front of you something new that you have made with your own hands. This in itself should give you self-confidence.

Now to return to the question of compound origami, I should like to give a few remarks about the best approach to it. As I have said, compound origami is generally used when the form of the thing you are trying to represent is complicated. In general, this means forms that have many pointed parts like crab, deer, insects, and certain flowers. In a following section, I shall teach you a few basic forms that are tools to use in creating the pointed parts of such forms without any trouble; but before doing so I must discuss the way in which you ought to divide the parts of the object you want to produce in compound origami. This division is not always made on the basis of the sizes or areas of the parts alone. On the contrary, the most important thing is to discover which of the parts characterize the object and to divide the total shape in such a way as to give emphasis to these distinctive traits. For example, large wings characterize the seagull; long, slender legs and neck the giraffe; and black back and white belly the penguin. Sometimes, considerations other than mere shape are the outstanding features that require emphasis. In the case of the crab, rather than the presence

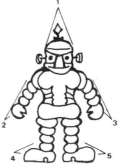

of eight legs, the animal's habit of walking sideways deserves attention. In making origami airplanes, balance is most important. You can see, then, that these various points—often different for each new object—are the things that require development. The origami in the charts at the top of the page are all folded from single pointed elements. I think that they represent the characteristic traits well enough for you to recognize them at once, even without the labels.

The line drawings on the page are simple representations of some models with indications of the number of pointed elements needed to express them in origami terms. Models of this simple design format clearly reveal the route to follow in analyzing and devising origami. Though, in nature, insects have six legs, the number is not requisite in some origami cases. Similarly, if an origami figure represents a bird in flight, there is no need to show the legs. The kneeling deer is a very simple form. It is essential in all these cases to identify the characteristic feature. For instance, try to discover wherein the form of the pigeon differs from that of the swan, the shape of the grasshopper from that of the praying mantis. After you have accurately grasped the outstanding traits of the animal, decide how best to fold the paper to give these characteristics vivid representation. Then you will be able to analyze the object in terms of number of pointed parts needed and finally select the basic origami forms that suit your needs.

Basic Origami Forms

Although the number of recognized basic origami forms is great, as I have said, knowledge of more forms—or more techniques—than you can readily apply is useless. For that reason, I have limited the basic forms here to six, all of which are fundamentally important because of their numbers of sharp points. I have included two forms with four points. It is true that in this respect the two are the same, but since different folding methods produce different characteristics, each of the forms might be selected for individual reasons. Furthermore, both are well known forms that I found it difficult to omit. In the preceding section, I said that analyzing an image in terms of the number of pointed elements needed to represent it in origami makes the creative process easier. The basic forms given here are limited to a maximum of four points. What happens then if the form you want to develop requires five or six points? For instance, a four-legged beast might require four points for the legs, one for the head, another for the tail, and perhaps two for the ears. What to do in such cases? I think on the basis of my earlier discussion, you will already have guessed that the answer to the question is compound origami made up of two of the basic forms. With compound origami you can handle six- or seven-pointed figures with ease.

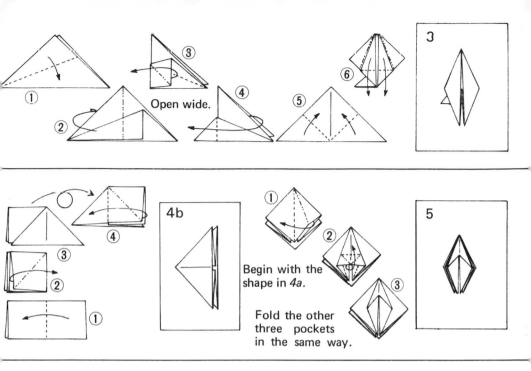

Open wide.

Begin with the shape in *4a*.

Fold the other three pockets in the same way.

But what if even compound origami fails to provide enough pointed parts? Give up the attempt to represent such figures in origami. To repeat myself, good origami has beauty of form and is not excessively complicated. These conditions of origami merit will not evolve from the mere attempt to recreate the physical shape of a thing. First, grasp and thoroughly understand the most striking characteristics of the object then concentrate your creative efforts on recreating those traits. This is the correct way to true origami creativity.

Perhaps the most striking proof of this approach is to be found in some traditional Japanese origami figures that have been popular for centuries. On the following pages, I present a few of the most outstanding of these origami. I hope that you will try your hand at folding them, even if you have seen or perhaps made them before.

23

Some Masterpieces of Traditional Origami

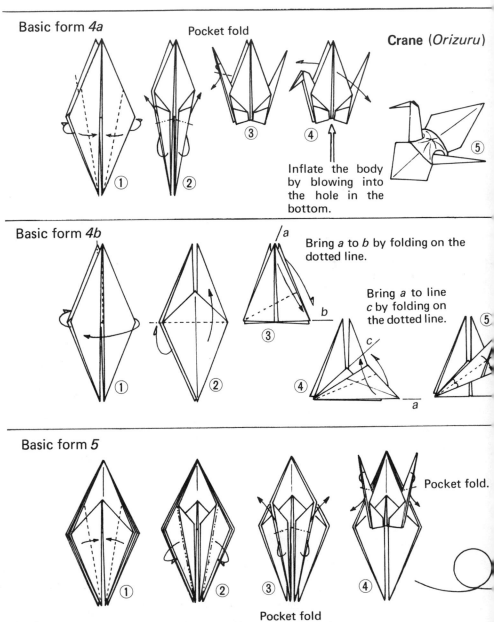

Basic form *4a*

Pocket fold

Crane (*Orizuru*)

③ ④

Inflate the body by blowing into the hole in the bottom.

⑤

Basic form *4b*

Bring *a* to *b* by folding on the dotted line.

③

Bring *a* to line *c* by folding on the dotted line.

④ ⑤

① ②

Basic form *5*

Pocket fold.

① ② ③ ④

Pocket fold

The crane, which has become a virtual symbol of all origami, is a variation on the true form of the living bird; but it nonetheless gives a striking sense of the beautiful creature. In other words, the origami captures the essence of the crane. The other two origami on this page —the *Orihazuru*, or crane with folded wings, and the Frog—have long given great happiness because of their eternal freshness and unchanging loveliness. All three of these masterpieces represent the rich emotional experiences of origami masters of the past. They are part of the origami heritage and as such deserve to be made with thought and care.

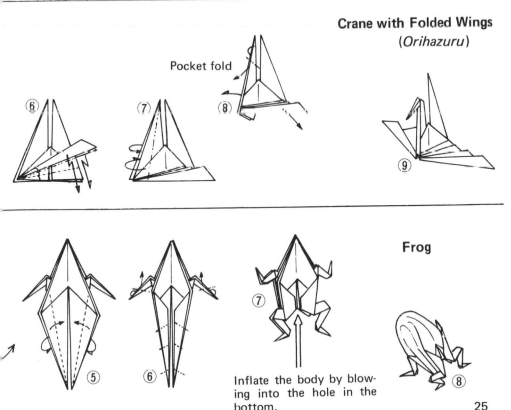

Crane with Folded Wings
(*Orihazuru*)

Pocket fold

Frog

Inflate the body by blowing into the hole in the bottom.

25

Let me thank you for having read Chapter One. I realize that at the beginning learning basic steps is sometimes a nuisance; but once that stage has been passed, great pleasure awaits you. I trust that for the rest of the book, from Chapter Two, **The Toy Box**, through the section on masks and human figures you will enjoy the distinctive pleasure that origami can give.

The Toy Box

Vehicles, Ornaments, and Other Things

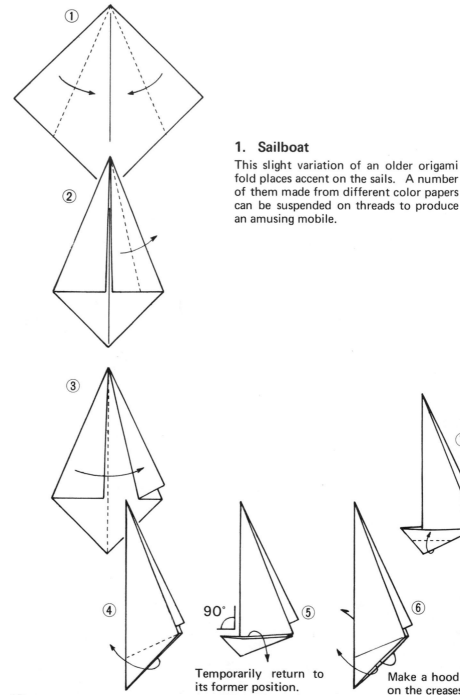

1. Sailboat

This slight variation of an older origami fold places accent on the sails. A number of them made from different color papers can be suspended on threads to produce an amusing mobile.

90°

Temporarily return to its former position.

Make a hood fo on the creases.

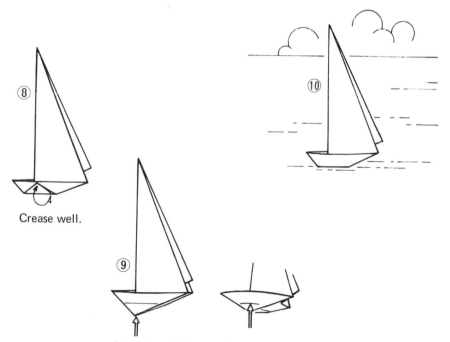

⑧

Crease well.

⑨

Insert by folding on these creases.

⑩

Houses

Church

2. Warehouse

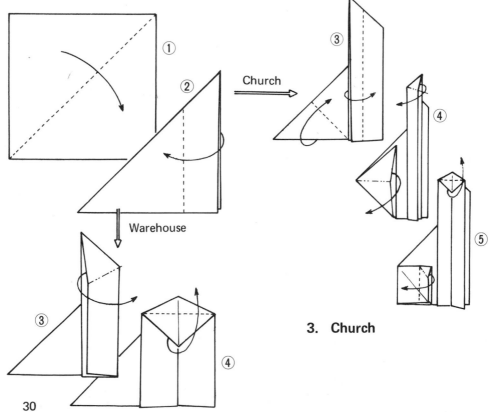

① ②

Church ⟹

③ ④

Warehouse

③ ④

⑤

3. Church

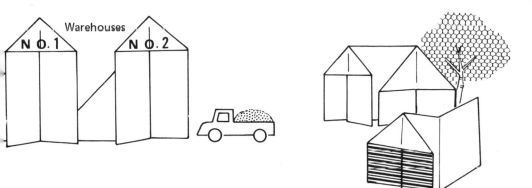

Warehouses

N O.1 **N O.2**

Make a miniature town for your
children's miniature automobiles.

Garage

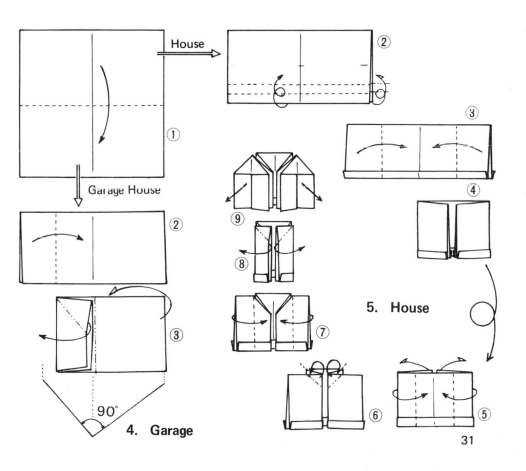

House

Garage House

1

2

3

4

90°

4. Garage

9

8

7

6

5

5. House

31

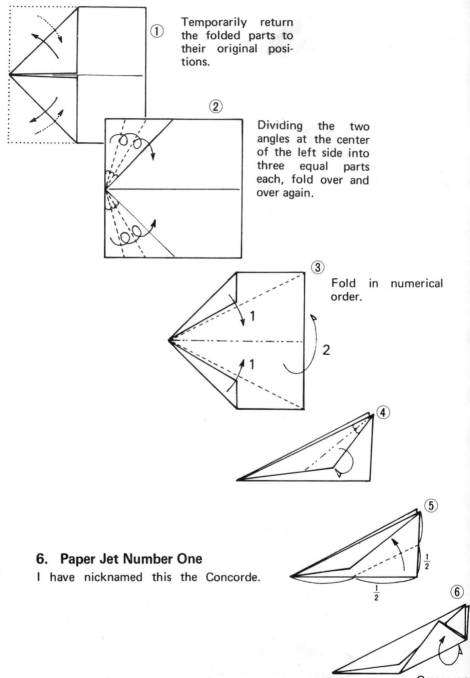

① Temporarily return the folded parts to their original positions.

② Dividing the two angles at the center of the left side into three equal parts each, fold over and over again.

③ Fold in numerical order.

④

⑤

⑥

6. Paper Jet Number One
I have nicknamed this the Concorde.

Crease well

32

Paper airplanes are a source of immense pleasure; they give me—and I suppose many of my readers—great relaxation, even though they are airborne for only a few seconds. Making them, however, often presents difficulties. For instance, a plane that flies perfectly well when made of one kind of paper, will not fly at all made from a paper of a different weight or quality. Sometimes it is necessary to twist the wings or perform other adjustments to improve performance characteristics.

As a rule, rectangular paper is considered better for paper airplanes because this shape results in more accurate positioning of the nose and hence flight direction. But I have developed what I think are good fliers using square paper. The five models that I introduce in the next few pages are the result of about a month's experimentation and of strict selection on the basis of performance. I hope that they will help you relax in moments of stress.

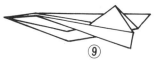

⑨

⑦ Using the creases made in the preceding step, make a pocket fold.

⑧

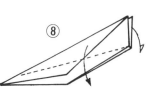

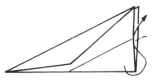

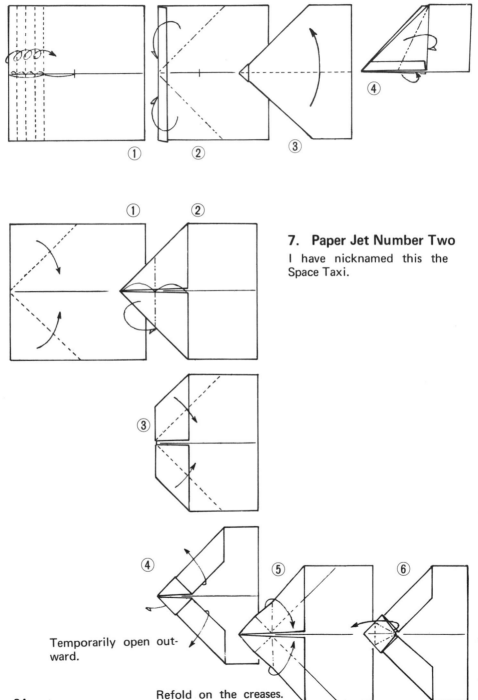

7. Paper Jet Number Two

I have nicknamed this the Space Taxi.

Temporarily open outward.

Refold on the creases.

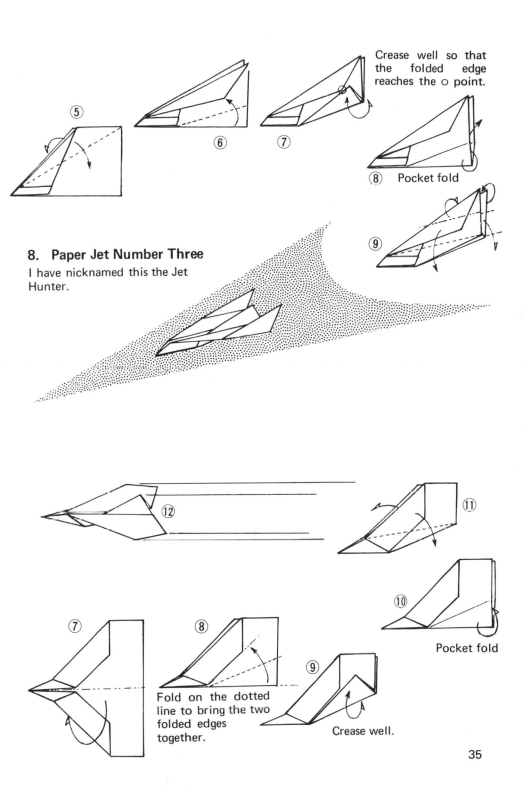

⑤

⑥

⑦

Crease well so that the folded edge reaches the o point.

⑧ Pocket fold

⑨

8. Paper Jet Number Three

I have nicknamed this the Jet Hunter.

⑫

⑪

⑩

Pocket fold

⑦

⑧

Fold on the dotted line to bring the two folded edges together.

⑨

Crease well.

9. Moon Rocket

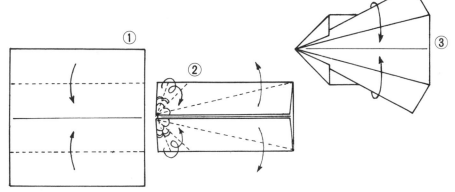

10. Sky Yacht

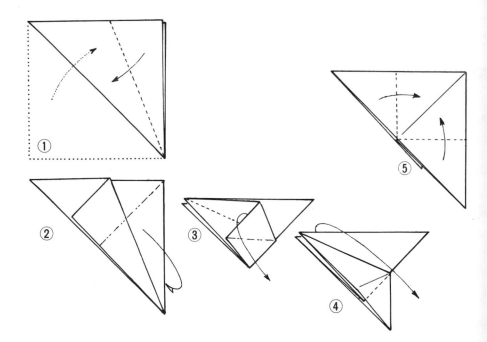

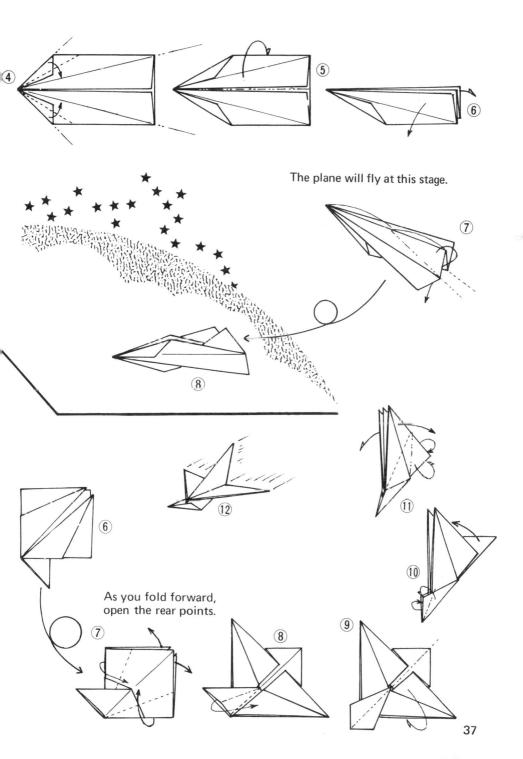

④ ⑤ ⑥

The plane will fly at this stage.

⑦

⑧

⑥

⑫

⑪

⑩

As you fold forward,
open the rear points.

⑦ ⑧ ⑨

37

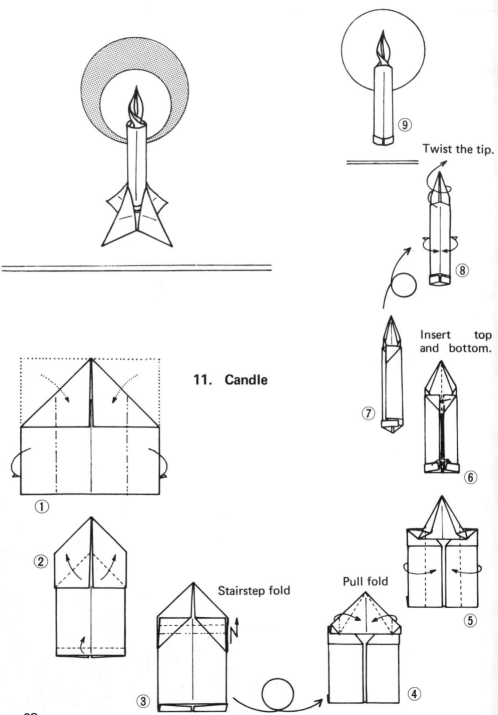

11. Candle

①

②

③ Stairstep fold

④ Pull fold

⑤

⑥ Insert top and bottom.

⑦

⑧ Twist the tip.

⑨

12. Candlestick

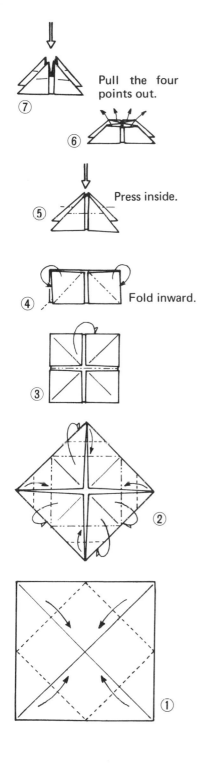

⑦

Pull the four points out.

⑥

⑤ Press inside.

④ Fold inward.

③

②

①

39

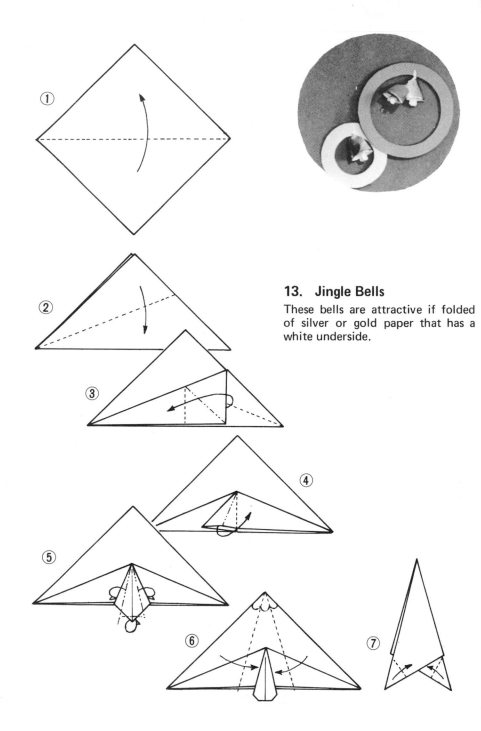

13. Jingle Bells

These bells are attractive if folded of silver or gold paper that has a white underside.

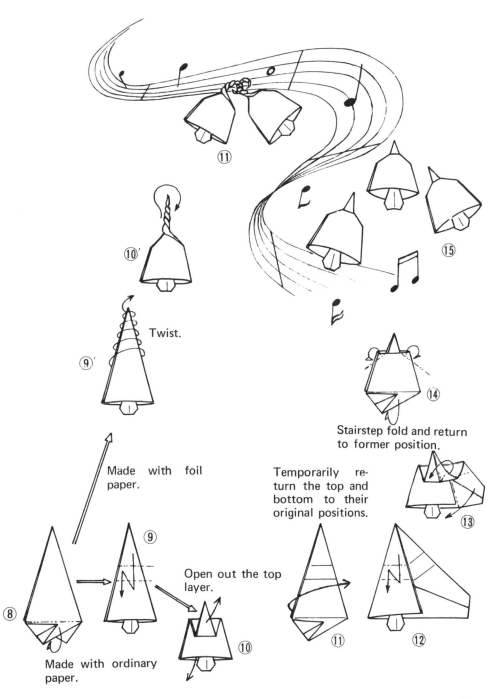

Twist.

Made with foil paper.

Open out the top layer.

Made with ordinary paper.

Temporarily return the top and bottom to their original positions.

Stairstep fold and return to former position.

Basic Form *4a*

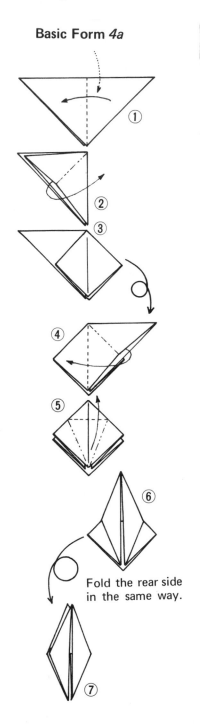

①
②
③
④
⑤
⑥
Fold the rear side in the same way.
⑦

The photograph on the right shows a classical Japanese origami called the "Chrysanthemum Dish." It is made with basic form *4a*, in which all points are folded into the center. By pulling two of the points, it is possible to pop the form into the Chrysanthemum-dish shape. The same folds become beautiful stars made with foil paper with the silver or gold on the inner side.

① Begin with basic form *4a*.

② Valley fold on the dotted line, bringing the sides around in the directions shown by the arrows.

③

④

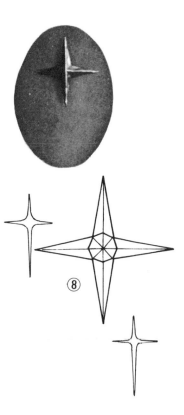

14. Stars

Like the jingle bells, these stars are effective made with gold or silver paper.

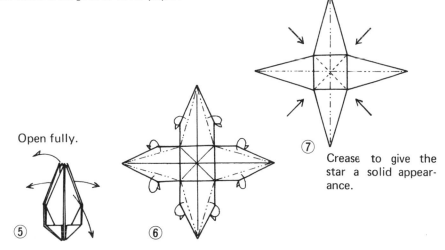

Open fully.

⑤

⑥

⑦

Crease to give the star a solid appearance.

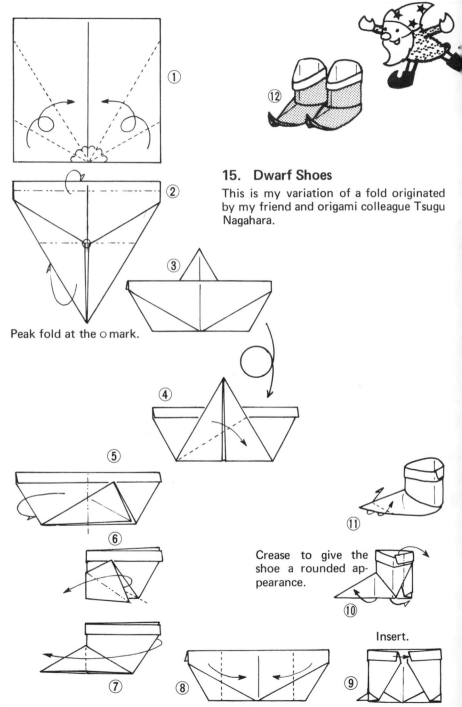

15. Dwarf Shoes

This is my variation of a fold originated by my friend and origami colleague Tsugu Nagahara.

Peak fold at the ○ mark.

Crease to give the shoe a rounded appearance.

Insert.

16.   Dwarf Hat

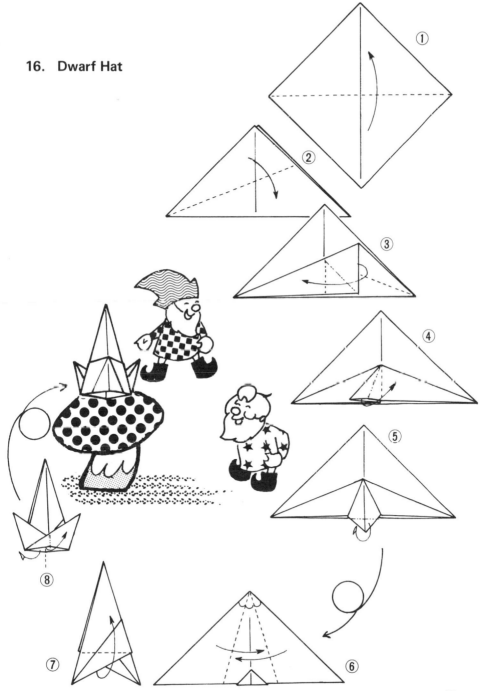

The contents of Chapter Two were largely directed toward amusing the children. I hope that you enjoyed making the folds and that you will find uses for the Christmas decorations contained in the latter part of the chapter.

As you have noticed, many basic forms and techniques were used in Chapter Two. The candle is one of the most difficult forms in the entire book to manage correctly. If you folded it well, the origami in the remaining chapters will be easy for you.

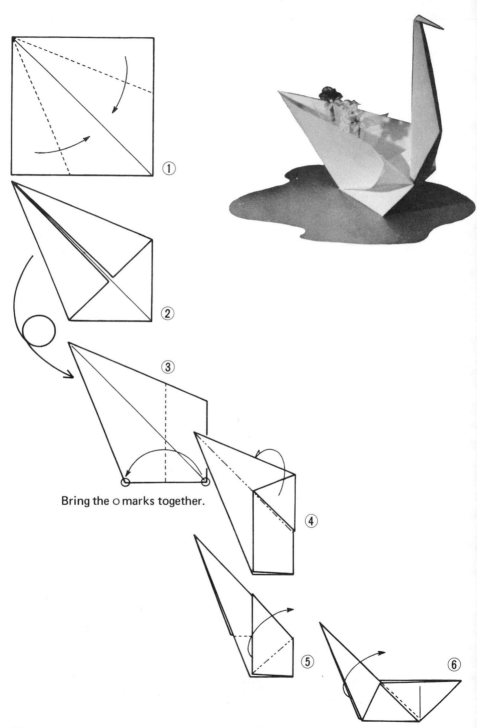

Bring the ○ marks together.

① ② ③ ④ ⑤ ⑥

This swan is especially effective made of pale-color paper. Once you have learned the folding method, try to execute steps *3* through *8*, making as few creases as possible. If you make the swan of slightly thick paper, it becomes an attractive container for dry flowers.

17. Swan

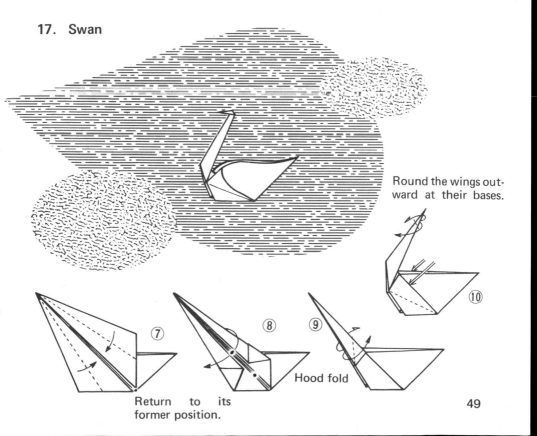

Round the wings outward at their bases.

⑩

⑦

⑧

⑨

Hood fold

Return to its former position.

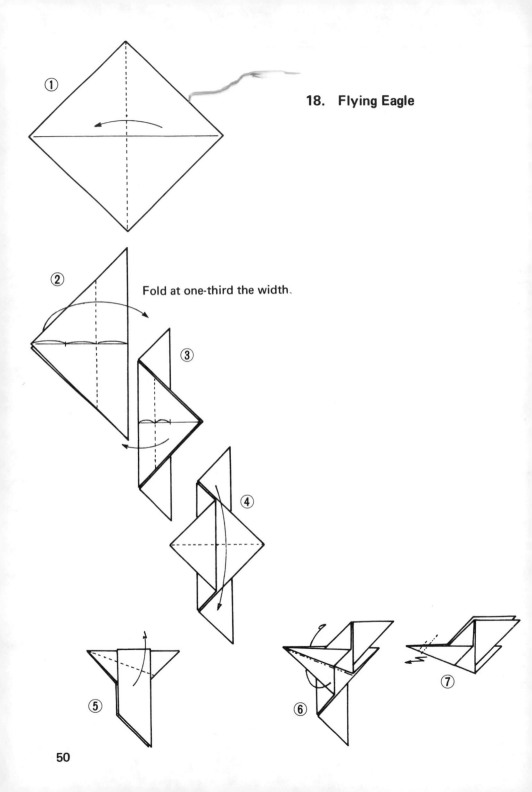

18. Flying Eagle

Fold at one-third the width.

Although I did not deliberately set out to make an eagle origami that will fly, if this one is held lightly in the fingers—as shown in the drawing—and released with a slight push, it will glide through the air. Children enjoy eagle races with these origami.

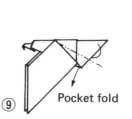

⑪

Make a small pocket fold to suggest the typical hook beak.

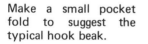

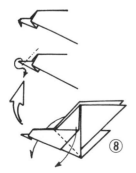

Pocket fold

⑨

⑧

⑩

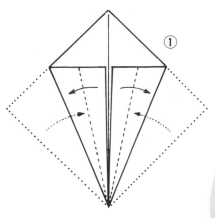

①

②

19. Peacock

③

④

⑤

Holding the figure firmly at the ○ mark, pull the bottom point upward in the direction of the arrow.

Make a pocket fold on the rear side like the one on the front.

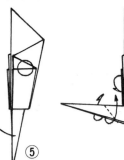

⑥

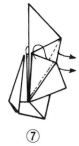

⑦

In attempting to express the gorgeous splendor of the peacock in simple origami folds, I tried many different ways, some of which are shown here. The fold explained in the drawings is one of those ways. Try to fold the others for yourself.

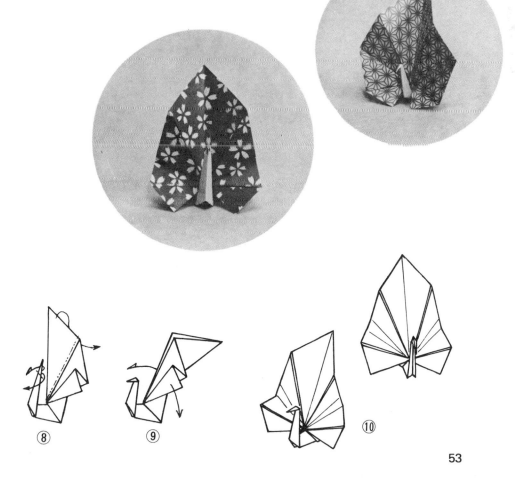

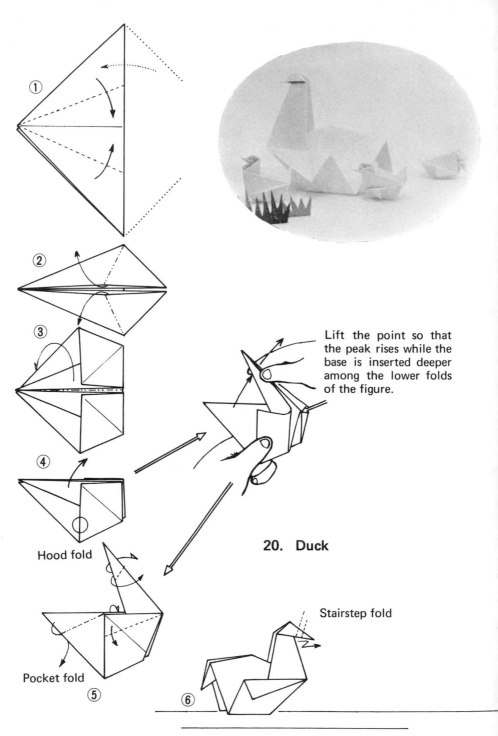

① ② ③ ④ Hood fold ⑤ Pocket fold ⑥

Lift the point so that the peak rises while the base is inserted deeper among the lower folds of the figure.

20. Duck

Stairstep fold

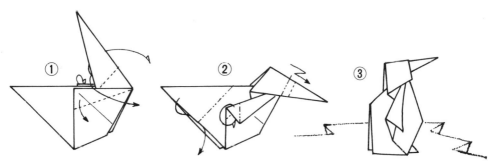

Begin with step *5* of the duck.

Make the duckling from a piece of paper one-fourth the size of that used for the duck.

21. Duckling

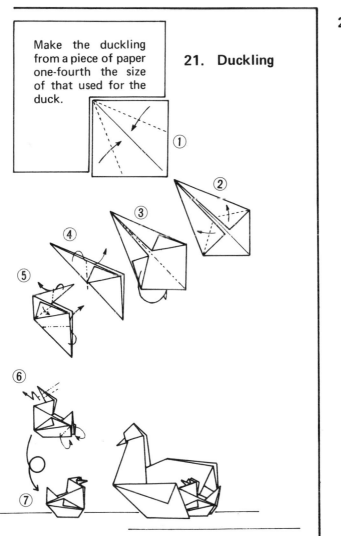

55

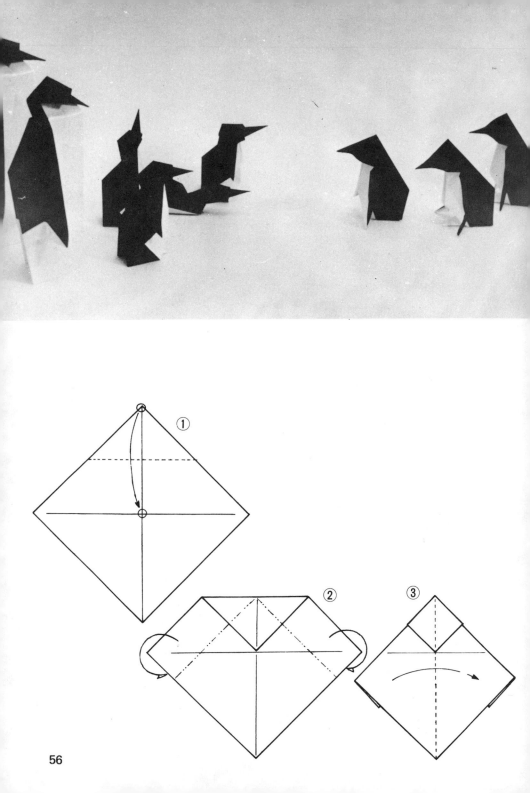

① ② ③

23. Penguin (II)

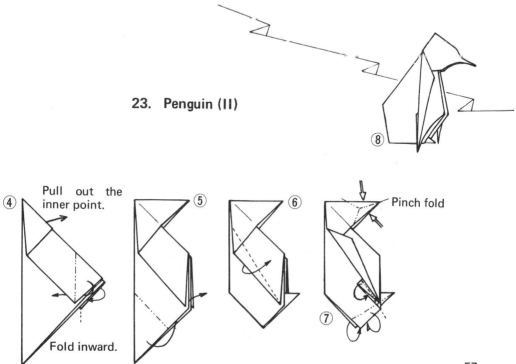

Pull out the inner point.

④

Fold inward.

⑤

⑥

⑦

Pinch fold

⑧

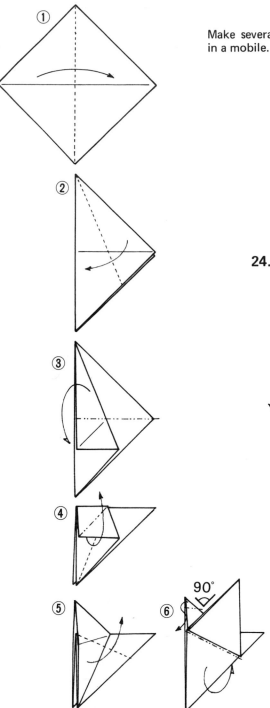

Make several pigeons and combine them in a mobile.

24. Pigeon in Flight

90°

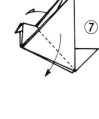

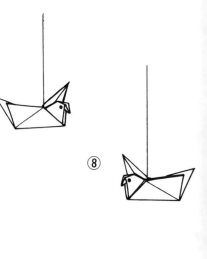

Begin with step 5 of the pigeon

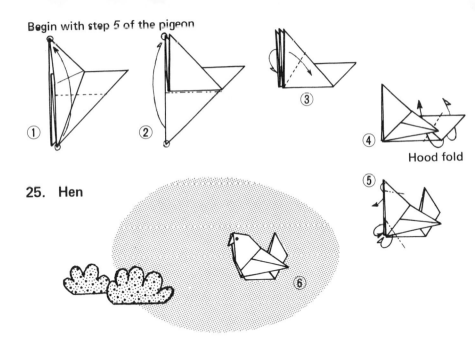

① ② ③

④ Hood fold

25. Hen

⑤

⑥

As the photograph shows, by altering the degrees of the angles and the sizes of the folds it is possible to convert the hen into a pigeon. Try the same kind of variation with other origami.

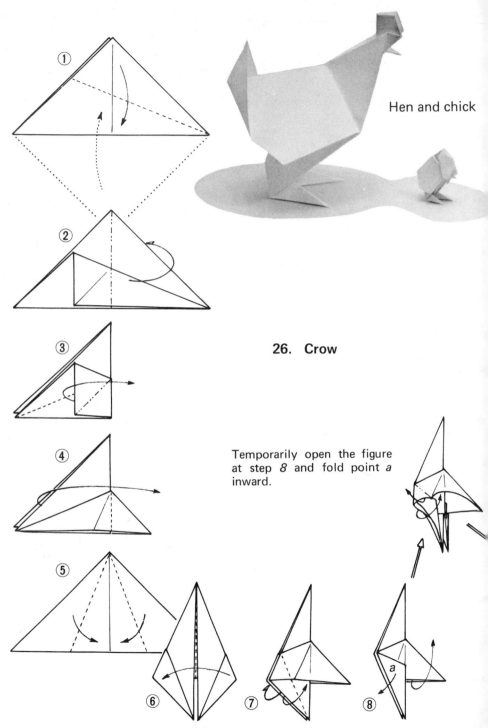

Hen and chick

26. Crow

Temporarily open the figure at step *8* and fold point *a* inward.

The photograph above shows variations in shapes; the photograph below reveals how altering poses can intensify interest.

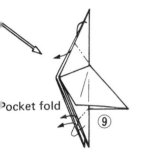

Pocket fold ⑨

⑩

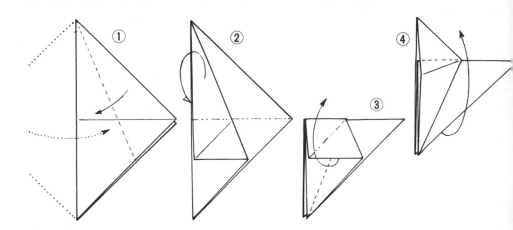

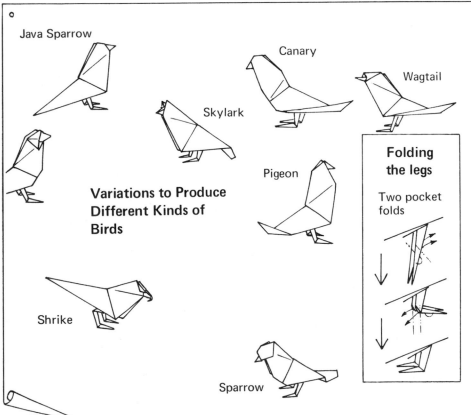

Java Sparrow

Canary

Wagtail

Skylark

Variations to Produce Different Kinds of Birds

Pigeon

Folding the legs

Two pocket folds

Shrike

Sparrow

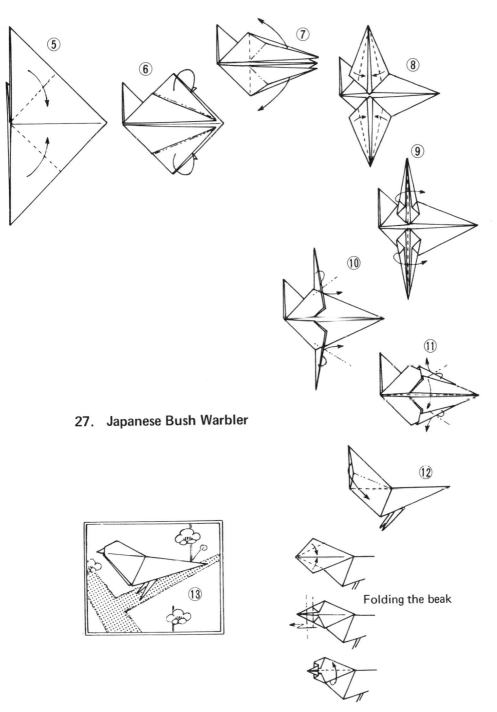

27. Japanese Bush Warbler

Folding the beak

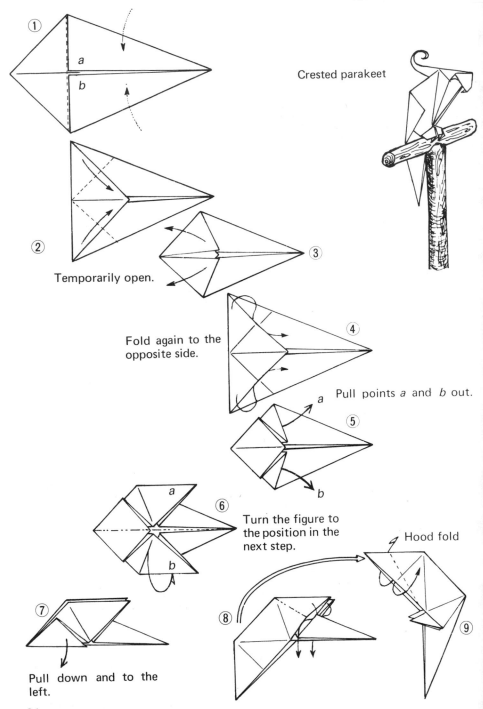

①

a

b

Crested parakeet

②

Temporarily open.

③

Fold again to the opposite side.

④

Pull points *a* and *b* out.

a

⑤

b

a

⑥

b

Turn the figure to the position in the next step.

Hood fold

⑦

⑧

⑨

Pull down and to the left.

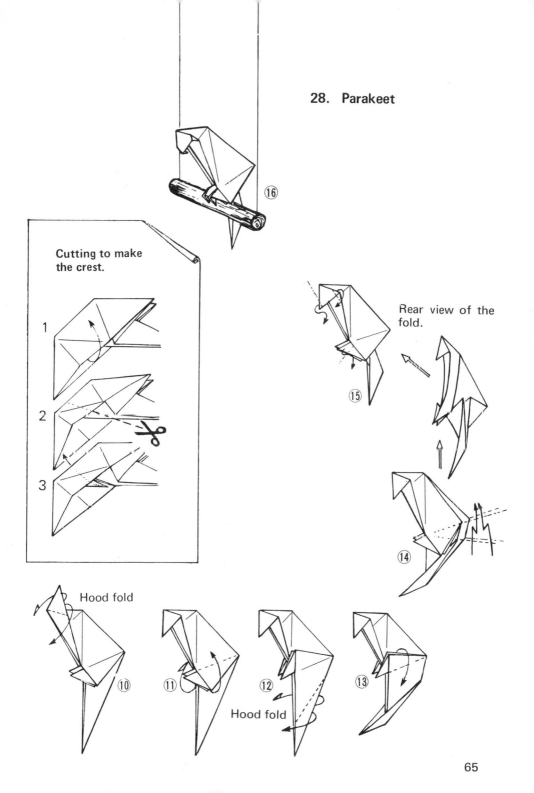

28. Parakeet

Cutting to make the crest.

1

2

3

Rear view of the fold.

⑯

⑮

⑭

Hood fold

⑩

⑪

⑫

Hood fold

⑬

Thousands of Birds

On the face of the earth today there exist roughly eight thousand species of birds. Origami is capable of close approximations of only a few of these. Obviously birds with pronounced characteristics like the penguin, ostrich, pelican, and parrot are relatively easy to deal with. The situation is much more difficult, however, when it comes to representing in origami terms the many birds whose general appearances are similar, like the sparrows and finches, the eagles and hawks, and the long-legged or wading birds. In such cases, you must concentrate on small details in order to approximate the distinctive looks of the creatures. The line drawings on pp. 59–62 show how this can be done. But bear in mind the fact that the true value of origami is not completely realistic representation. Furthermore, origami is not to be judged on the basis of whether it looks exactly like a given animal or object. For instance, if you like pigeons, analyze the appearance of the bird and try to recreate something pigeonlike in origami. Should a friend who sees your pigeon origami ask you if it is a sparrow, you need not be upset. Your work has clearly captured the mood of a bird, and that is sufficient. But if you want to convince your friend, invent an origami sparrow, show him the two together, and point out to him where he has made a mistake.

Insects and Flowers

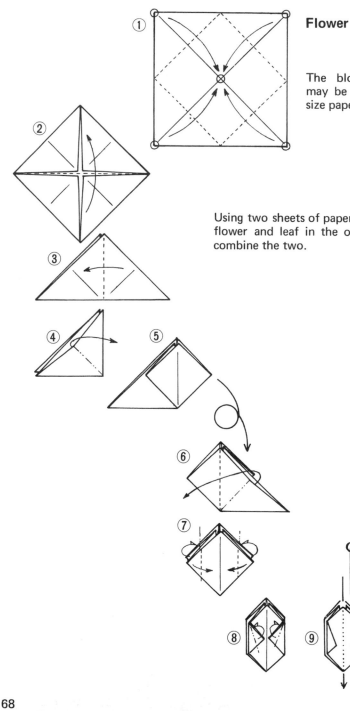

Flower

The blossom and leaves may be made of the same size paper.

Using two sheets of paper, make the tulip flower and leaf in the order shown and combine the two.

Make a small hole in the bottom of the flower. Blow into the hole to inflate the tulip. When combining the leaf and blossom, insert the stem into this hole.

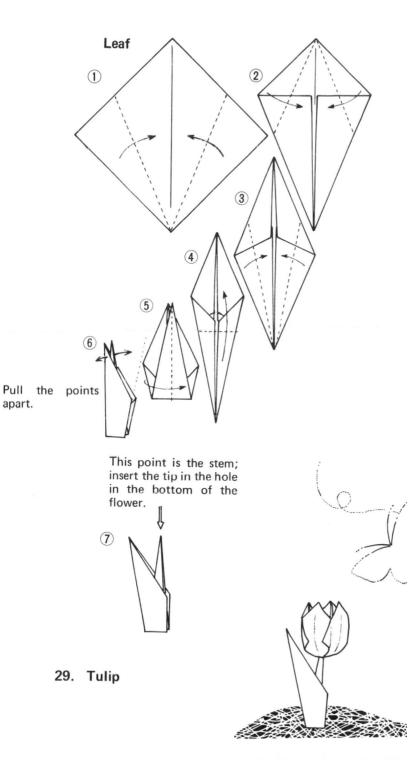

Leaf

① ② ③ ④ ⑤

⑥

Pull the points
apart.

This point is the stem;
insert the tip in the hole
in the bottom of the
flower.

⑦

29. Tulip

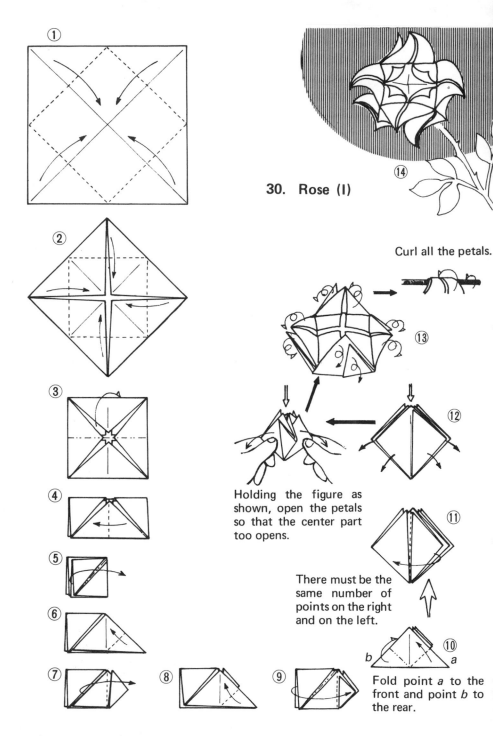

30. Rose (I)

Curl all the petals.

Holding the figure as shown, open the petals so that the center part too opens.

There must be the same number of points on the right and on the left.

Fold point *a* to the front and point *b* to the rear.

31. Rose (II)

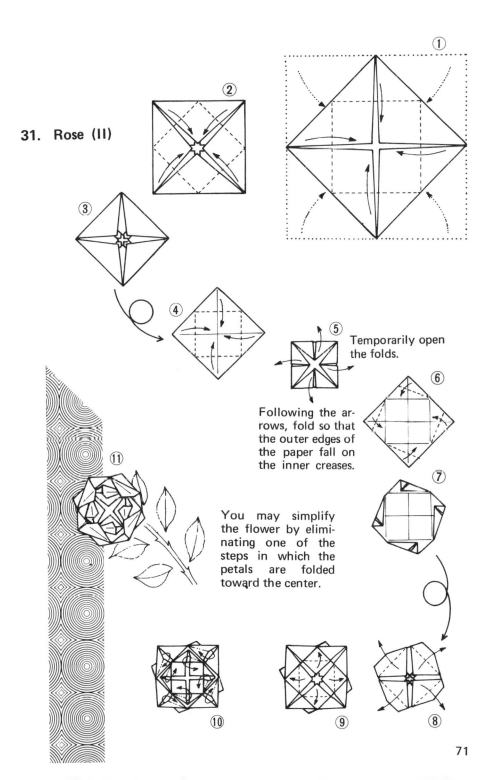

Temporarily open the folds.

Following the arrows, fold so that the outer edges of the paper fall on the inner creases.

You may simplify the flower by eliminating one of the steps in which the petals are folded toward the center.

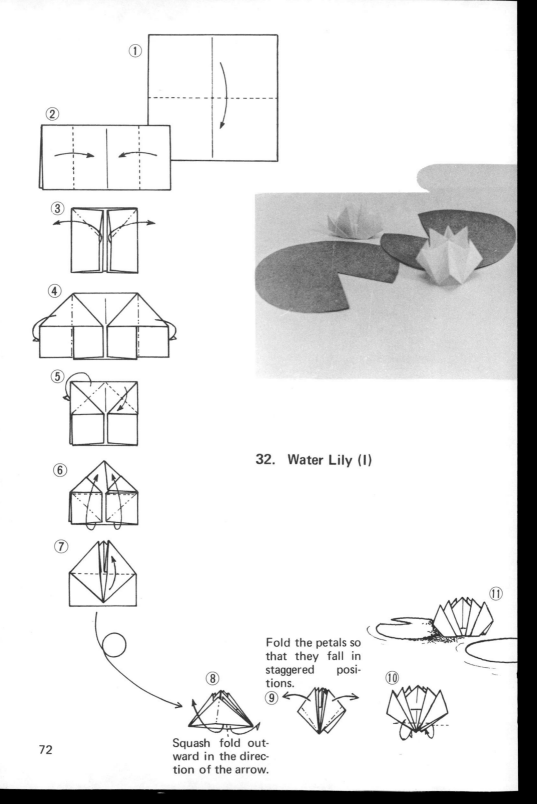

32. Water Lily (I)

Fold the petals so that they fall in staggered positions.

Squash fold outward in the direction of the arrow.

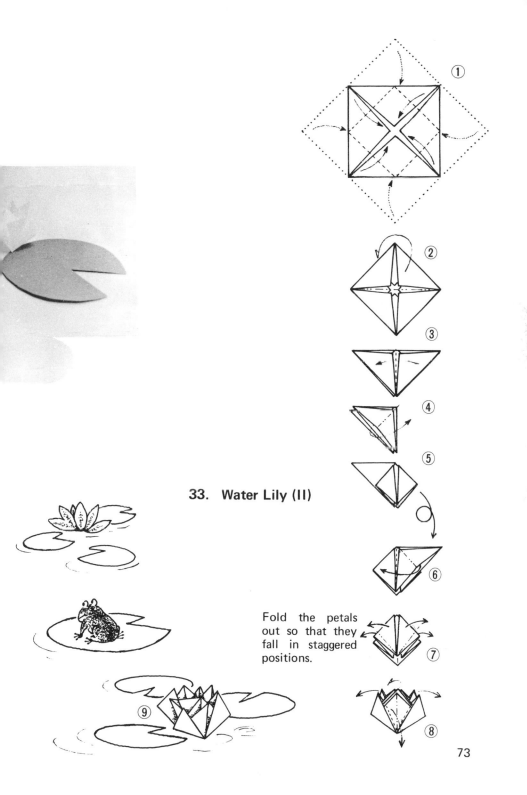

33. Water Lily (II)

Fold the petals out so that they fall in staggered positions.

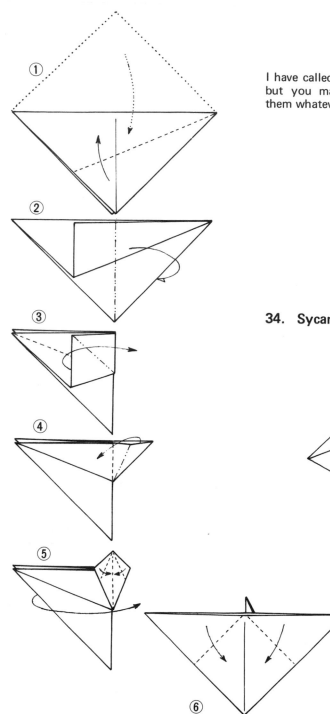

I have called these sycamore leaves, but you may vary them and call them whatever you like.

34. Sycamore Leaves

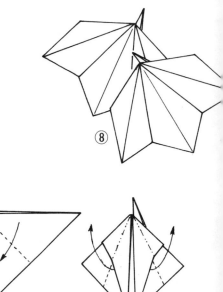

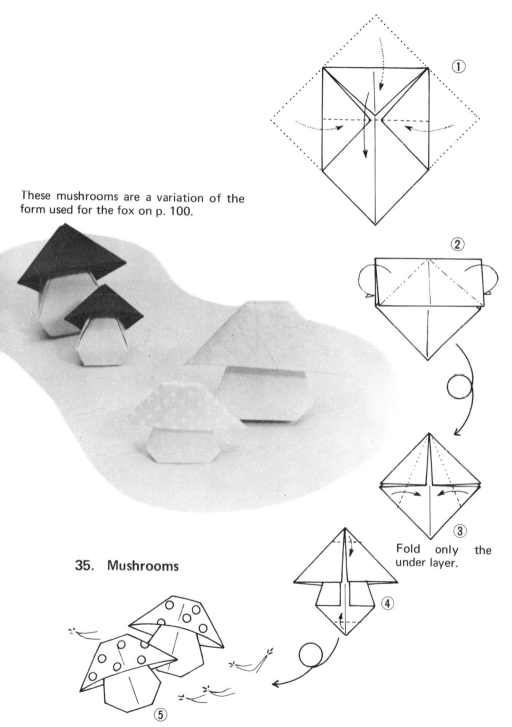

These mushrooms are a variation of the form used for the fox on p. 100.

①

②

Fold only the under layer.

③

35. Mushrooms

④

⑤

75

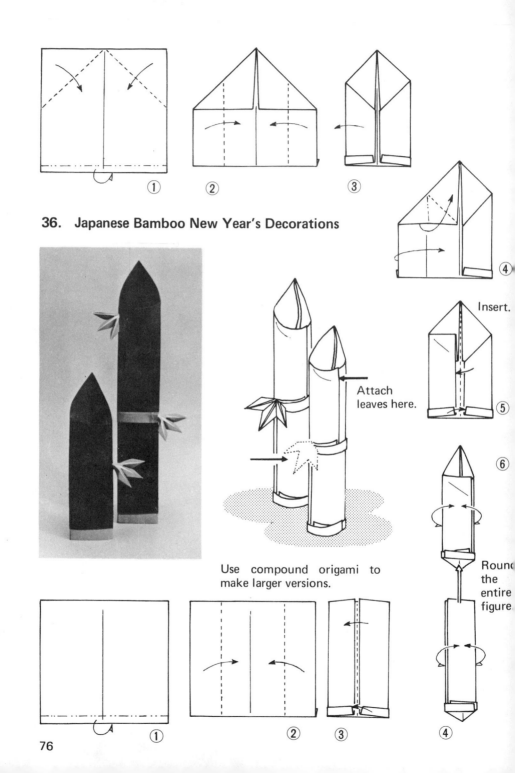

36. Japanese Bamboo New Year's Decorations

Attach leaves here.

Insert.

Round the entire figure.

Use compound origami to make larger versions.

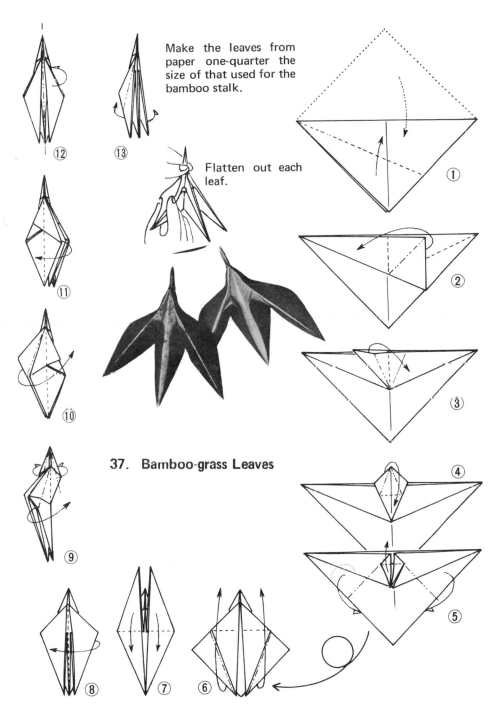

Make the leaves from paper one-quarter the size of that used for the bamboo stalk.

Flatten out each leaf.

37. Bamboo-grass Leaves

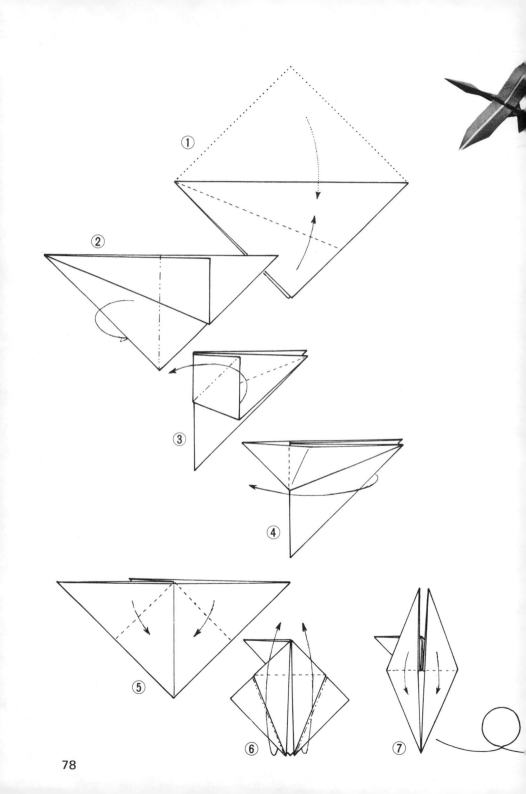

① ② ③ ④ ⑤ ⑥ ⑦

I call step *9* the basic insect form because it awakens many associations with other insect shapes.

(14)

38. Grasshopper

(13)

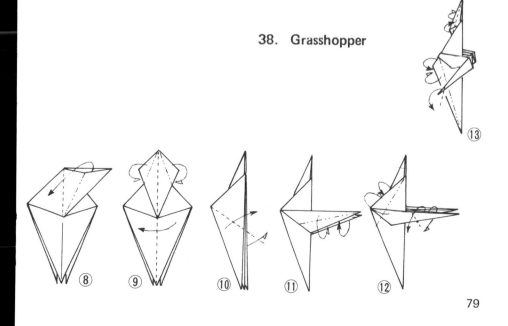

(8) (9) (10) (11) (12)

79

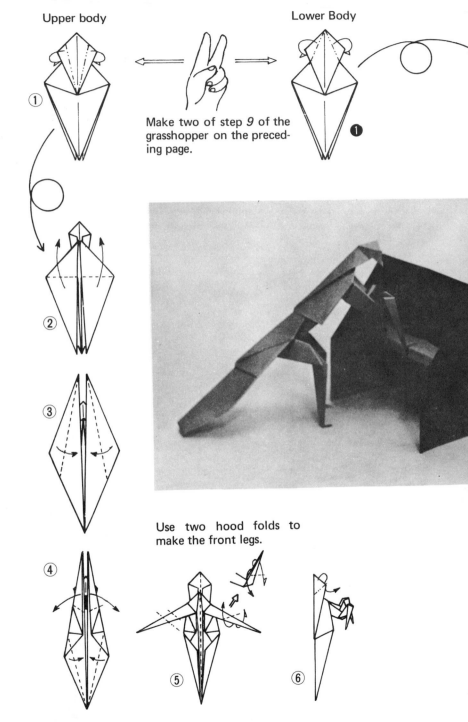

Upper body

①

Lower Body

①

Make two of step 9 of the grasshopper on the preceding page.

②

③

④

Use two hood folds to make the front legs.

⑤

⑥

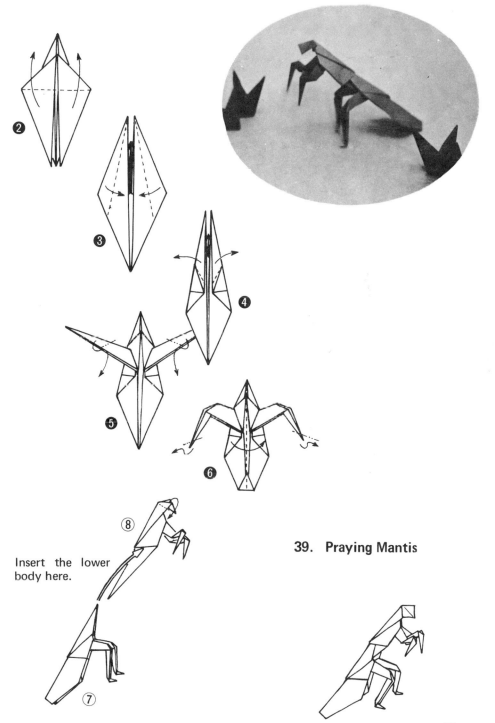

39. Praying Mantis

Insert the lower body here.

81

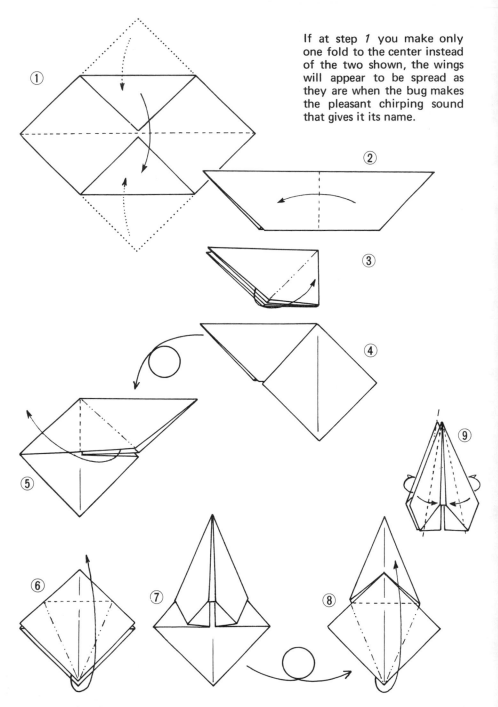

If at step *1* you make only one fold to the center instead of the two shown, the wings will appear to be spread as they are when the bug makes the pleasant chirping sound that gives it its name.

The long, slender antennae of the bug are essential to its appearance, but they are hard to make with folding techniques. Cut them from a separate piece of paper and glue them to the head.

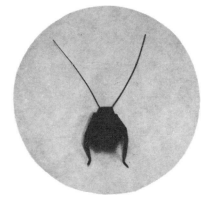

40. Bell Insect

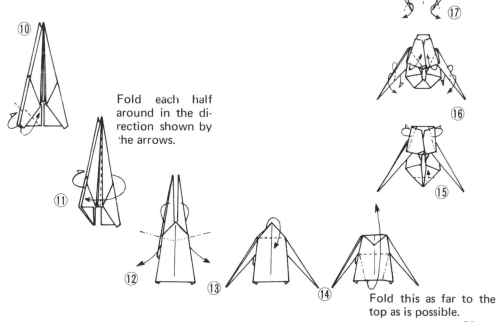

Fold each half around in the direction shown by the arrows.

Fold this as far to the top as is possible.

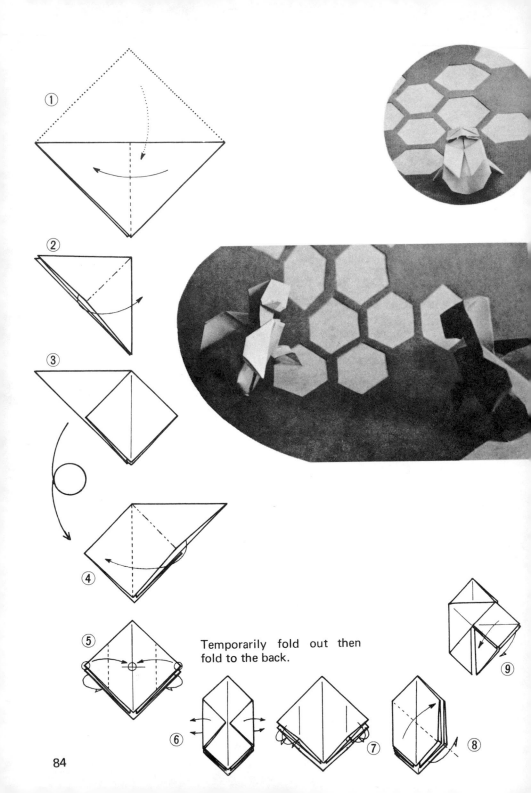

① ② ③ ④ ⑤

Temporarily fold out then fold to the back.

⑥ ⑦ ⑧ ⑨

84

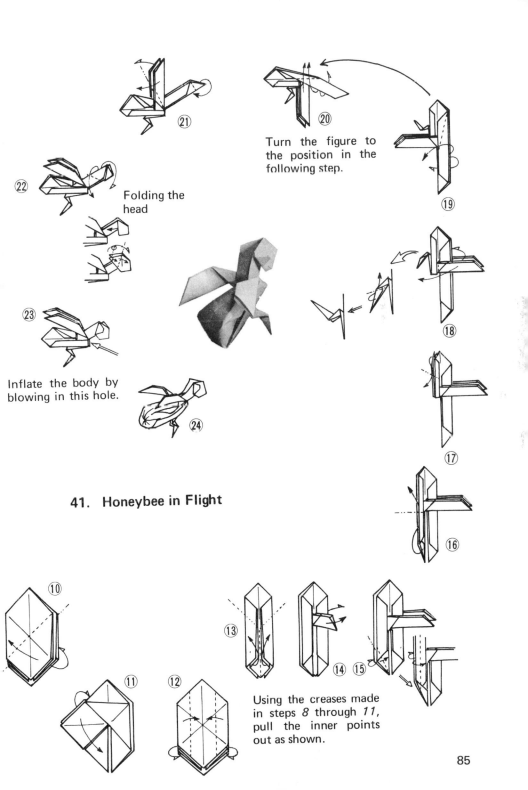

Turn the figure to the position in the following step.

Folding the head

Inflate the body by blowing in this hole.

41. Honeybee in Flight

Using the creases made in steps 8 through 11, pull the inner points out as shown.

Now that you have finished the chapter on plants and insects, you have dealt with the most difficult of all origami subjects. These two categories are hard to represent in origami because the inevitably straight folding lines do not lend themselves to the softness needed for flowers and because folding the elaborate bodies of insects is very complicated. Still, since plants and insects outnumber all other creatures living on the earth, we must try to use them as origami themes. Once again, however, do not try to approximate the appearance of the real things too closely. In other words, do not allow your origami flowers to look like commercial artificial blossoms and do not fold insects that are disagreeably ugly.

Water Creatures and Other Animals 5

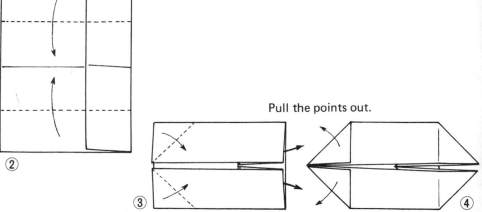

It is easy to make an origami rabbit that stands on its hind legs.

42. Rabbit

Toshio Chino, my respected senior origami colleague, has designed a rabbit that is among the finest of his works. I have taken the idea for my rabbit from his but have greatly simplified the folding method.

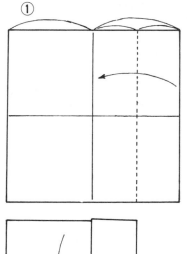

Pull the points out.

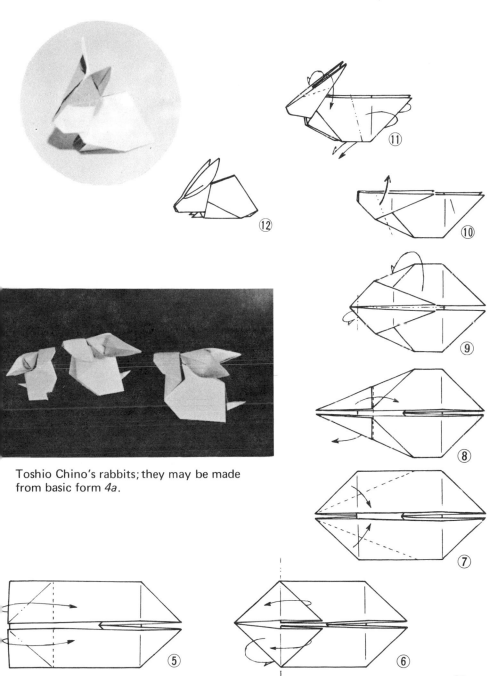

Toshio Chino's rabbits; they may be made from basic form *4a*.

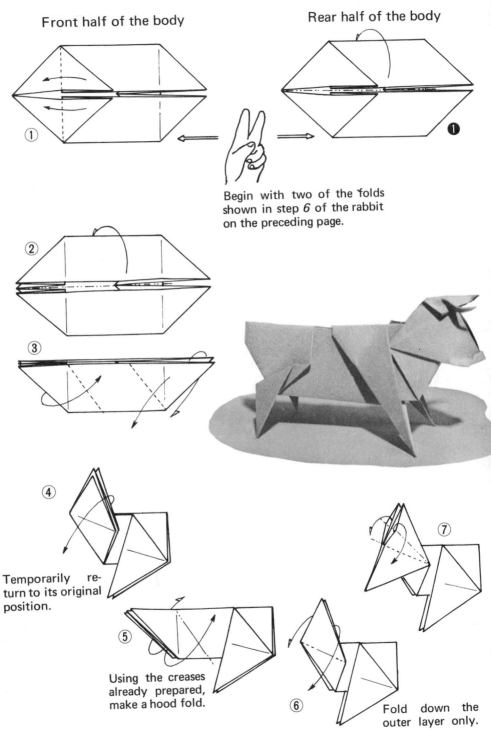

Front half of the body

Rear half of the body

①

❶

Begin with two of the folds
shown in step *6* of the rabbit
on the preceding page.

②

③

④

Temporarily re-
turn to its original
position.

⑤

Using the creases
already prepared,
make a hood fold.

⑥

⑦

Fold down the
outer layer only.

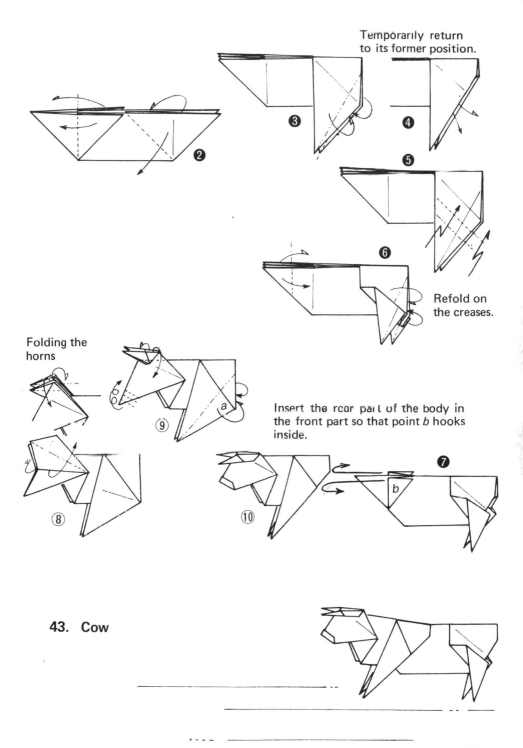

Temporarily return
to its former position.

❸

❹

❺

❻

Refold on
the creases.

Folding the
horns

⑨

⑧

Insert the rear part of the body in
the front part so that point *b* hooks
inside.

❼

a

b

⑩

43. Cow

Front half of the body

Rear half of the body

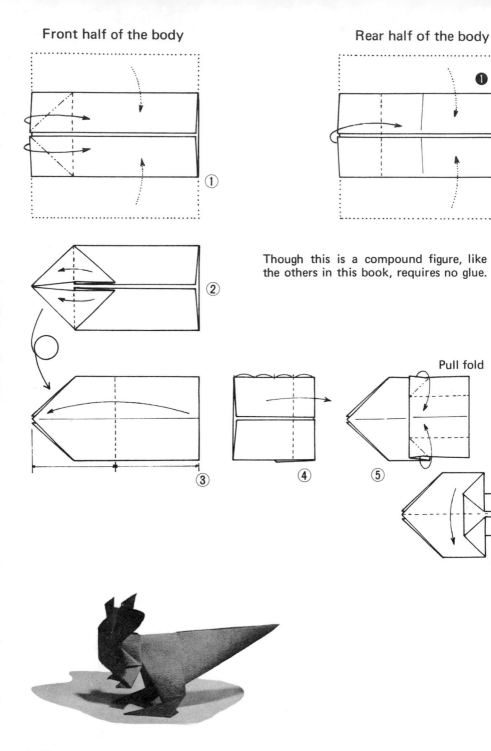

Though this is a compound figure, like the others in this book, requires no glue.

Pull fold

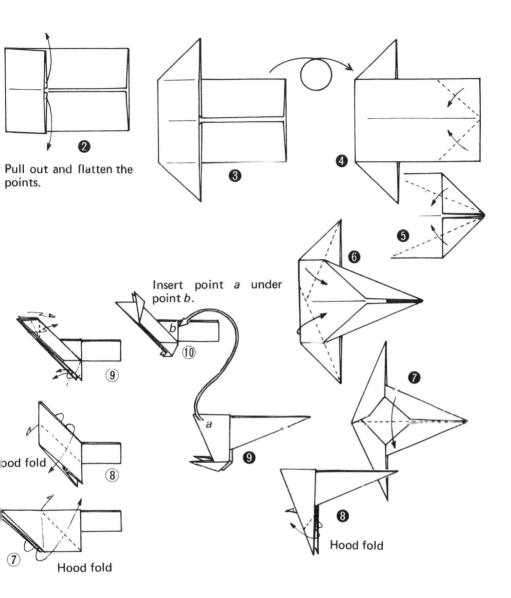

Pull out and flatten the points.

Insert point *a* under point *b*.

Hood fold

Hood fold

Hood fold

44. Kangaroo

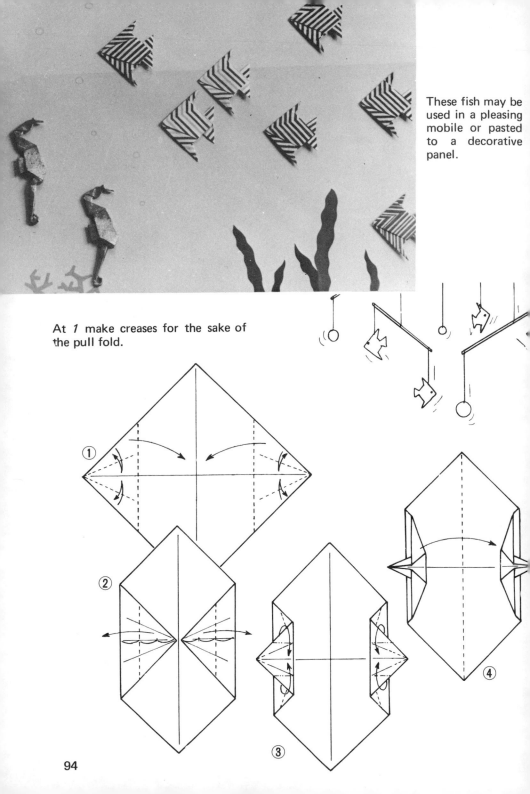

These fish may be used in a pleasing mobile or pasted to a decorative panel.

At *1* make creases for the sake of the pull fold.

① ② ③ ④

94

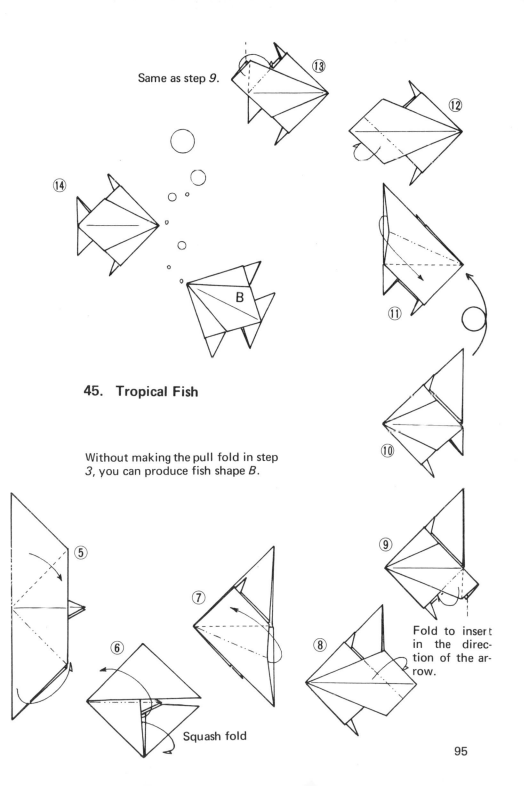

Same as step 9.

⑬

⑫

⑭

⑪

⑩

45. Tropical Fish

Without making the pull fold in step
3, you can produce fish shape B.

B

⑤

⑨

⑦

⑥

⑧

Fold to insert
in the direc-
tion of the ar-
row.

Squash fold

95

Upper half of the body   Lower half of the body

Compound

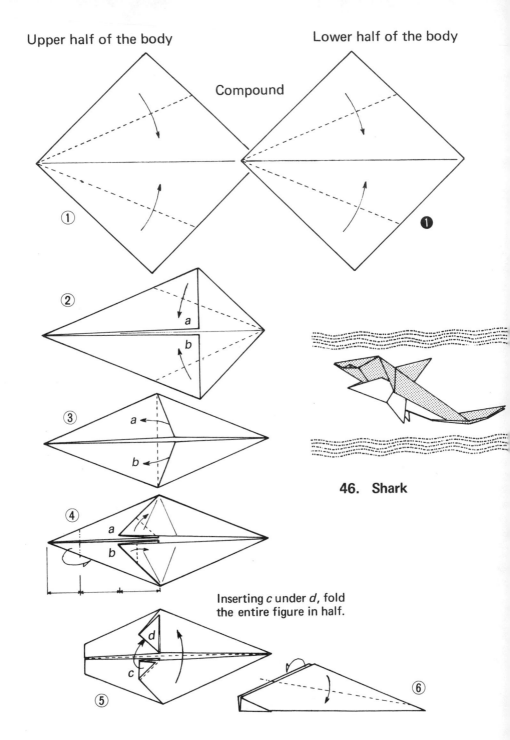

①   ❶

②   *a*   *b*

③   *a*   *b*

④   *a*   *b*

46. Shark

Inserting *c* under *d*, fold the entire figure in half.

⑤   *d*   *c*

⑥

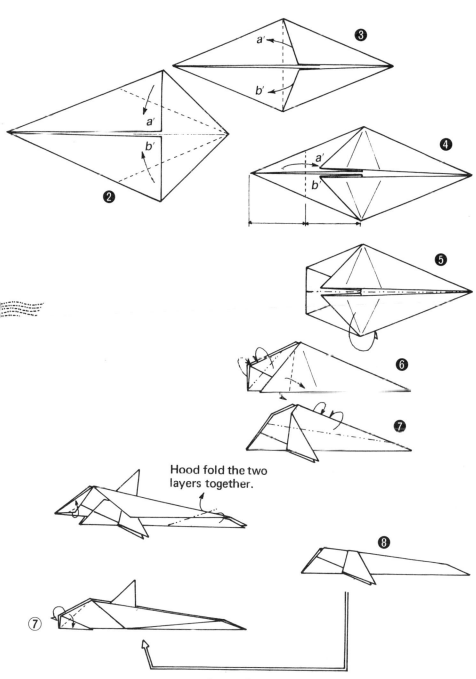

3

2

4

5

6

7

Hood fold the two layers together.

8

⑦

Insert *8* under *7*.

Made from only one sheet of paper, the frog looks like this.

Head   Body

Compound

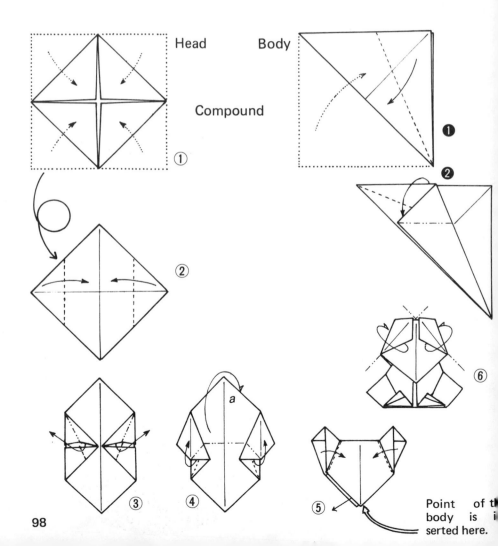

Point of the body is inserted here.

98

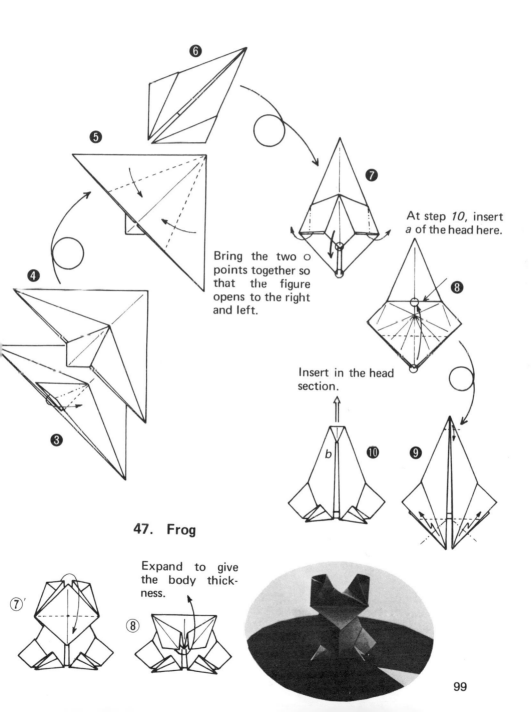

❻

❺

❹

❸

Bring the two ○ points together so that the figure opens to the right and left.

❼

At step *10*, insert *a* of the head here.

❽

Insert in the head section.

b ⑩ ❾

47. Frog

⑦′

Expand to give the body thickness.

⑧

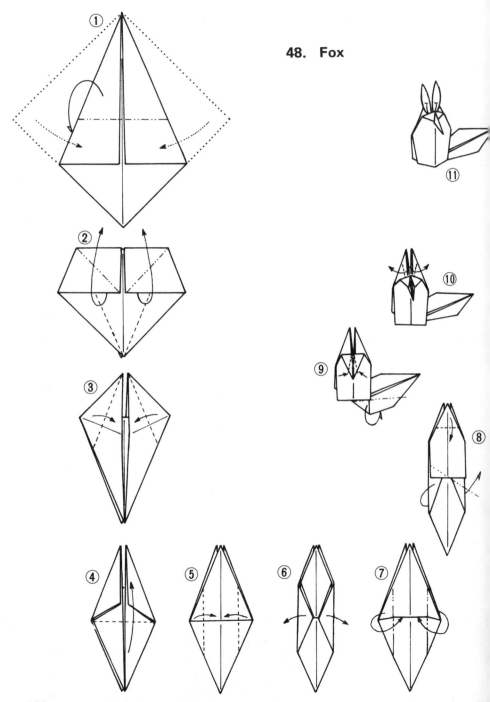

48. Fox

49. Snake

In Japanese children's stories, the snake, fox, and crow always play the parts of villains, but these origami are among my favorites.

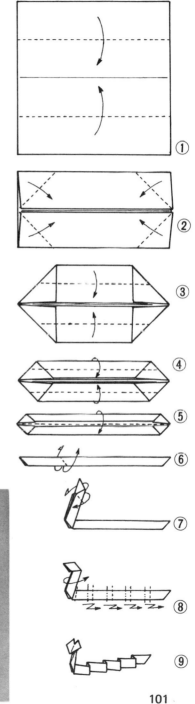

50. The Real Monster of Lake Ness

For many years, there has been talk of a great monster in the waters of Lake Ness but no one has advanced convincing descriptions of the creature. Here is my interpretation. It has two humps on its back, a long tail, a long, slender neck, and a tiny head. In fact, it looks very much like the dinosaurs of millions of years ago.

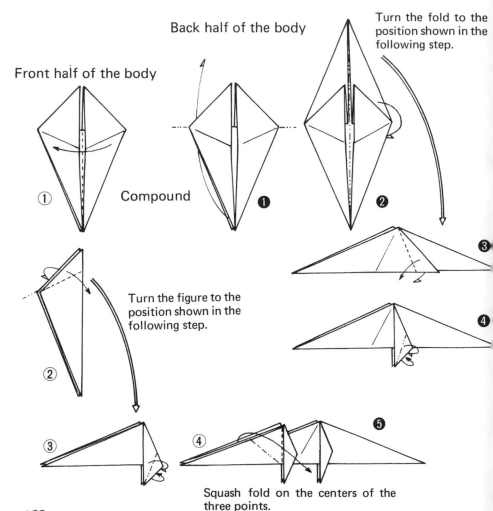

Front half of the body

Back half of the body

Turn the fold to the position shown in the following step.

Compound

Turn the figure to the position shown in the following step.

Squash fold on the centers of the three points.

Folding the head

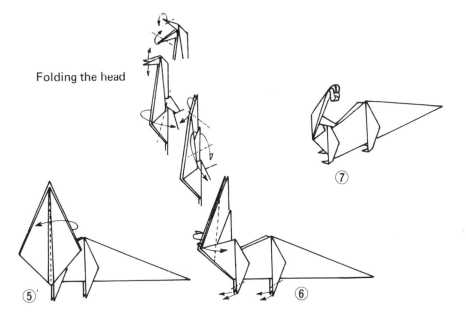

⑤

⑥

⑦

103

Head

Body

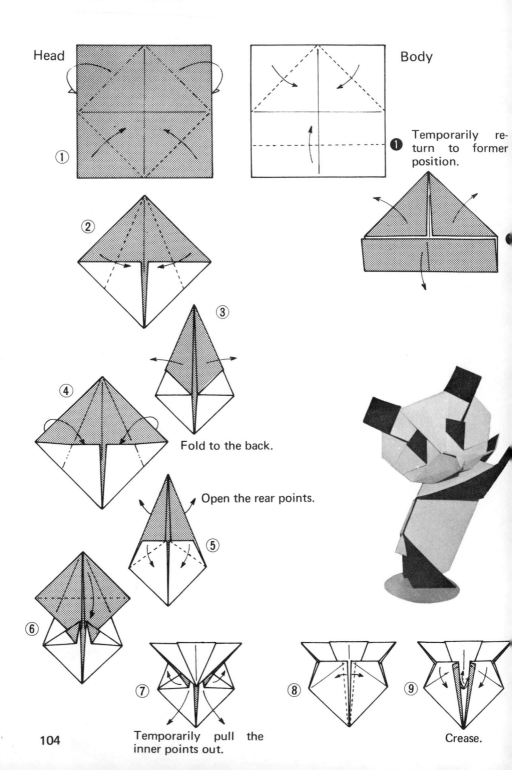

Temporarily return to former position.

① ②

③

Fold to the back.

④

Open the rear points.

⑤

⑥

⑦

Temporarily pull the inner points out.

⑧

⑨

Crease.

③

④

Bring *a* of step *12* here.

⑤

About 90 degrees.

51. Giant Panda

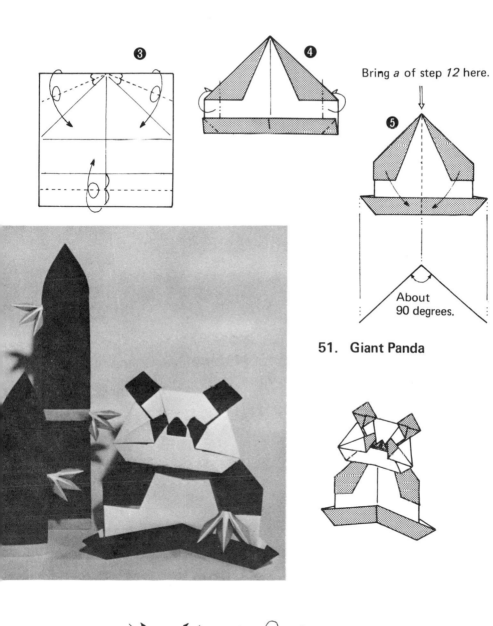

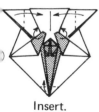
Insert.

⑪

⑫

⑬
Attach to the body.

Before moving to the last chapter, which deals with my favorite origami themes, I should like to say that, although I have made many origami in the animal, fish, and plant categories, I include in this book only the ones I am proudest of. I hope they will strike a spark of creative desire in you. I have offered the Giant Panda because, although the animal is found wild only in China, its charming appearance has long captured the hearts of children and adults everywhere.

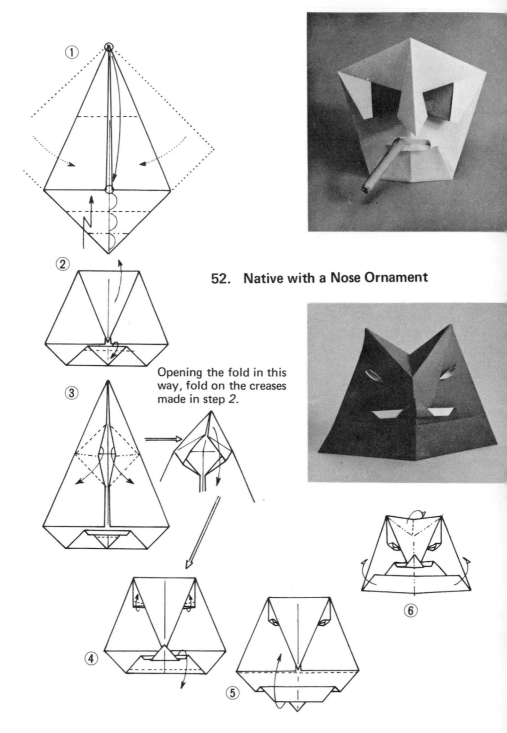

52. Native with a Nose Ornament

Opening the fold in this way, fold on the creases made in step 2.

53. Gang Boss Lurking in a Dark Street

If this mask looks like someone you know, you might be wise to change the title to something like The Face of a Wealthy and Happy Man.

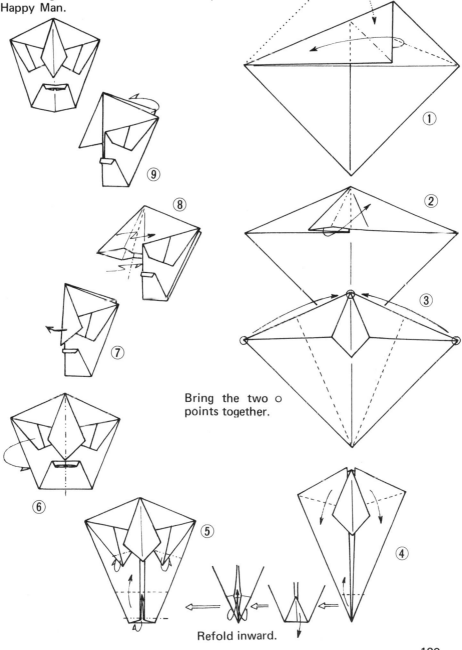

Bring the two o points together.

Refold inward.

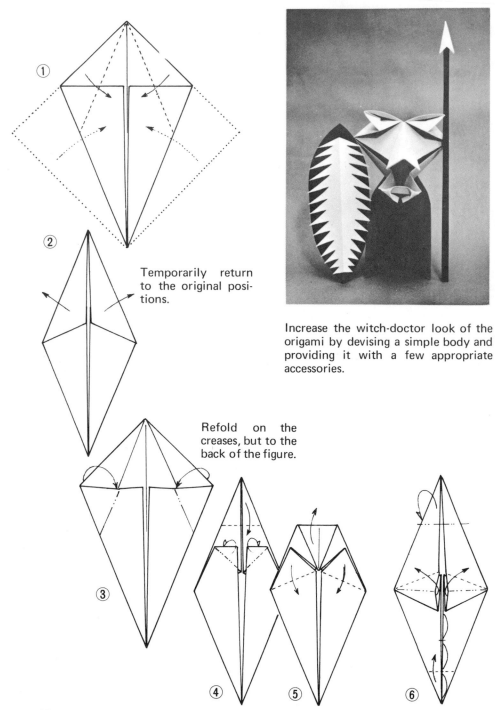

①

② Temporarily return to the original positions.

Increase the witch-doctor look of the origami by devising a simple body and providing it with a few appropriate accessories.

Refold on the creases, but to the back of the figure.

③

④ ⑤ ⑥

110

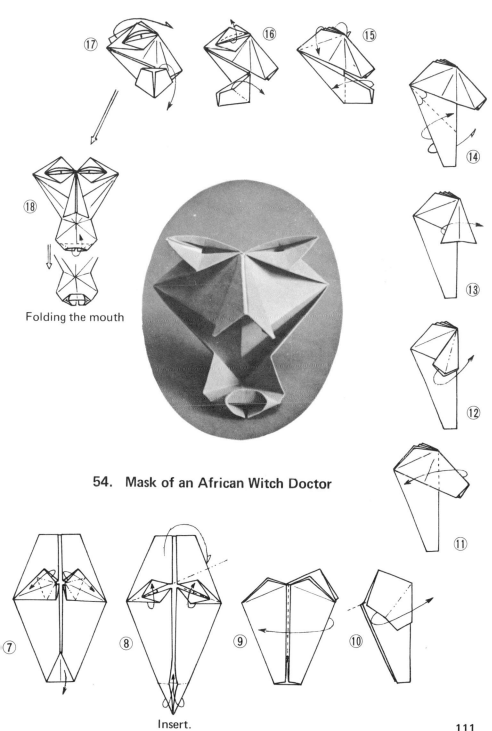

Folding the mouth

54. Mask of an African Witch Doctor

Insert.

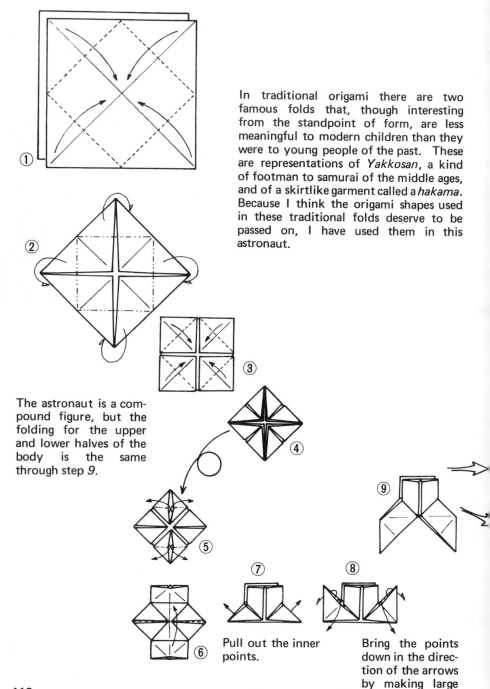

In traditional origami there are two famous folds that, though interesting from the standpoint of form, are less meaningful to modern children than they were to young people of the past. These are representations of *Yakkosan*, a kind of footman to samurai of the middle ages, and of a skirtlike garment called a *hakama*. Because I think the origami shapes used in these traditional folds deserve to be passed on, I have used them in this astronaut.

The astronaut is a compound figure, but the folding for the upper and lower halves of the body is the same through step *9*.

Pull out the inner points.

Bring the points down in the direction of the arrows by making large hood folds.

55. Astronaut

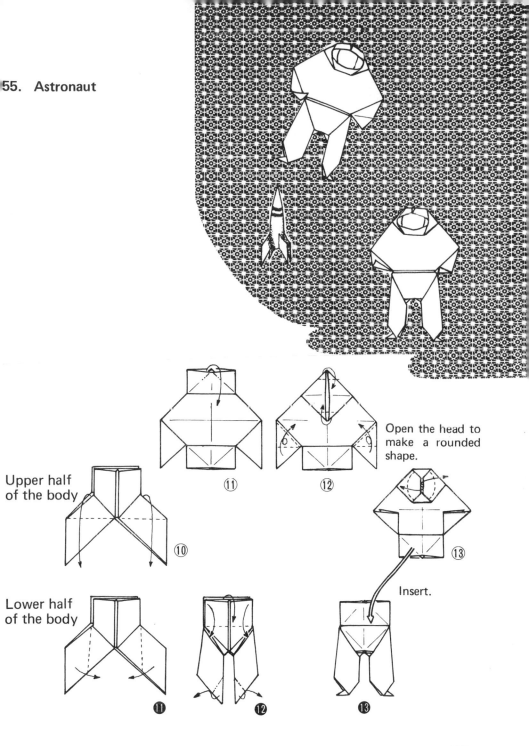

Upper half
of the body

⑩

Lower half
of the body

⑪

⑪

⑫

Open the head to
make a rounded
shape.

⑫

⑬

Insert.

⑬

113

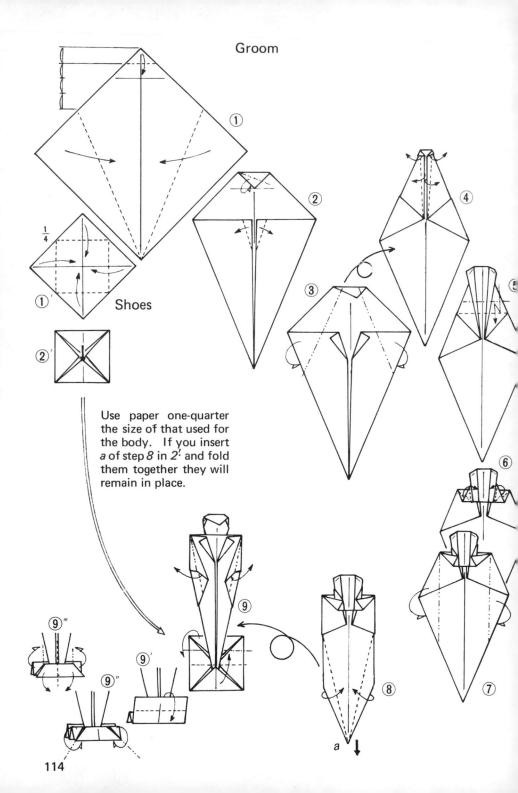

Groom

Shoes

¼

Use paper one-quarter
the size of that used for
the body. If you insert
a of step *8* in *2'* and fold
them together they will
remain in place.

114

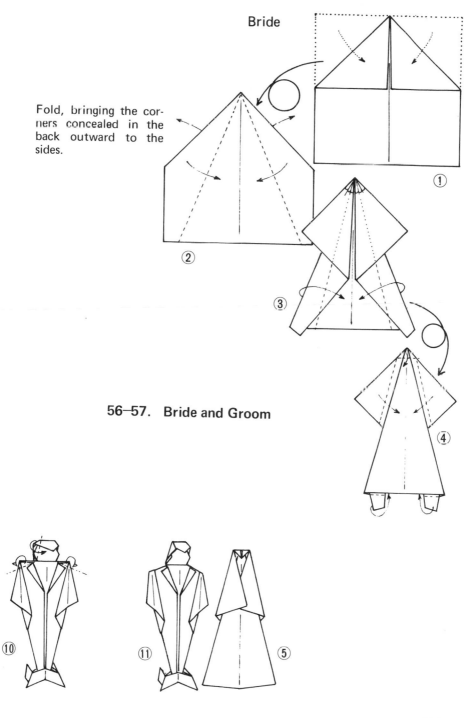

Bride

Fold, bringing the corners concealed in the back outward to the sides.

① ② ③ ④ ⑤ ⑩ ⑪

56–57. Bride and Groom

The top fold should be about
one-quarter of the way from
the corner to the center of
the sheet.

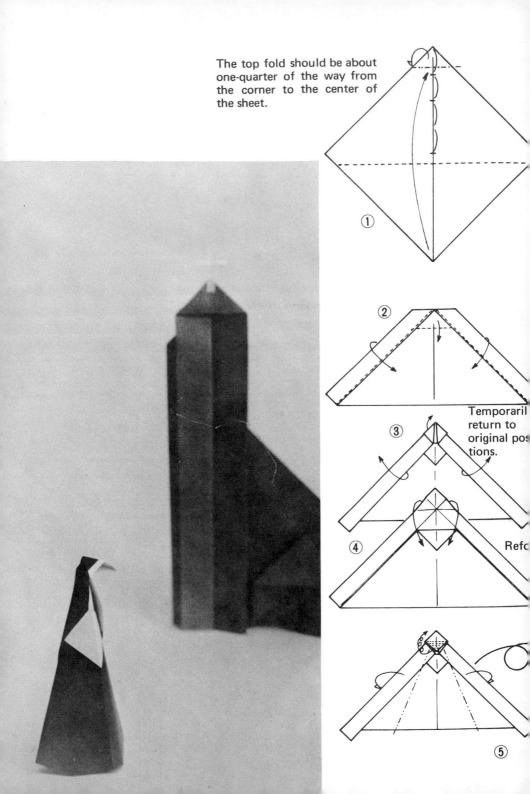

①

②

③

Temporaril
return to
original pos
tions.

④

Refo

⑤

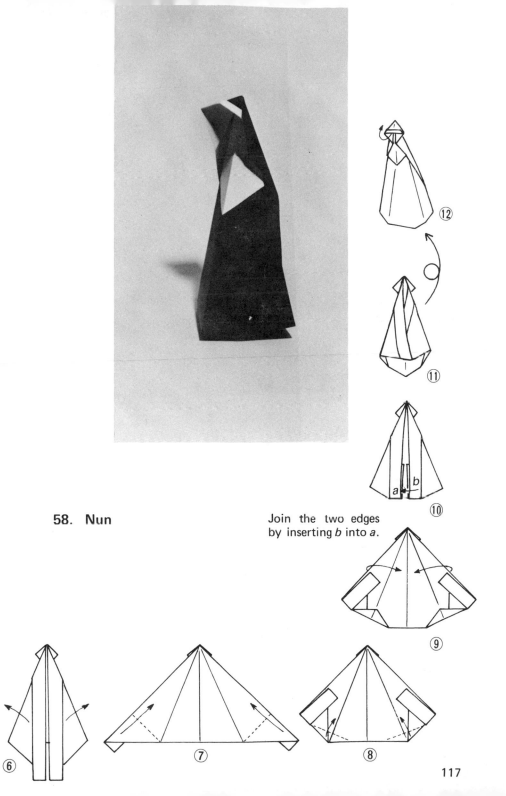

58. Nun

Join the two edges
by inserting *b* into *a*.

An angel made by Toshio Chino from rectangular paper

⑩

59. Angel

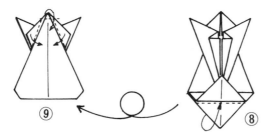
⑨   ⑧   ⑦

For this angel, as for the rabbit on p.88, I have taken hints from the works of origami artist Toshio Chino.

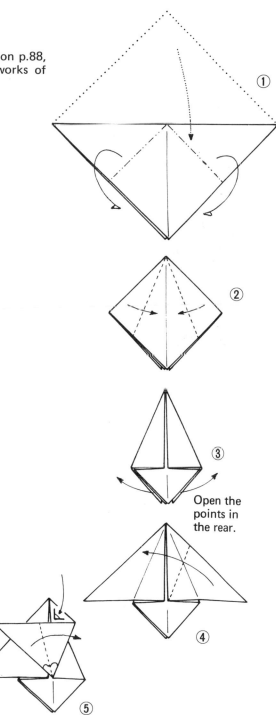

①

②

③

Open the points in the rear.

④

Fold the left side as you folded the right one.

⑥

⑤

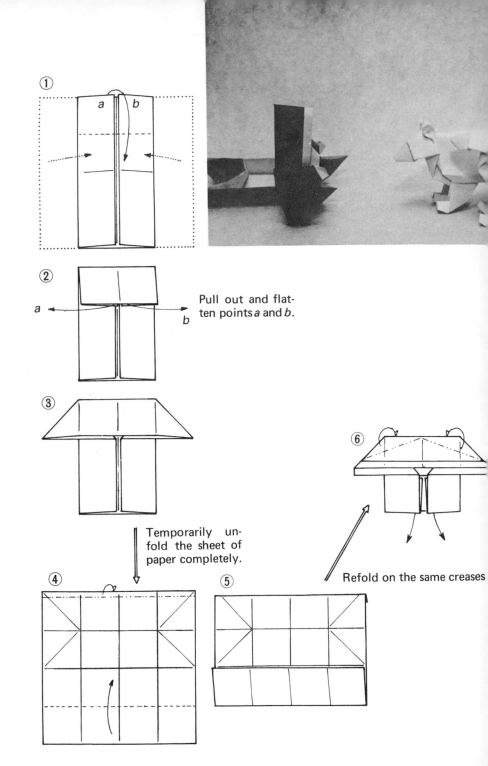

①

②

a ← → b

Pull out and flatten points *a* and *b*.

③

⑥

Temporarily unfold the sheet of paper completely.

④

⑤

Refold on the same creases

Working from step *10*, you can make eskimos if you use your ingenuity.

60. Babies

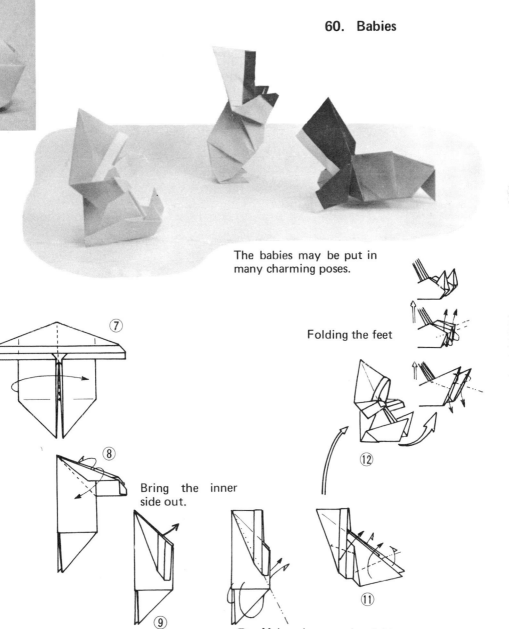

The babies may be put in many charming poses.

Folding the feet

⑦

⑧

Bring the inner side out.

⑨

⑩ Make a large pocket fold.

⑪

⑫

61. Arabian

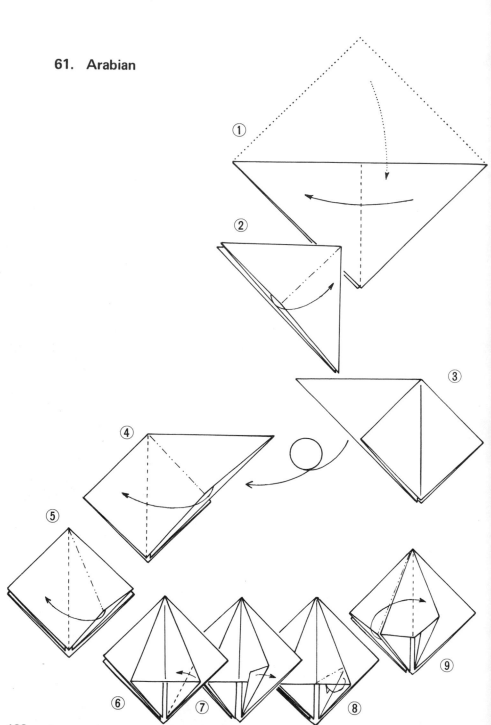

Using this figure as a basic element, I once made a scene from the Arabian Nights to show in an exhibition. Why not try making one of your own?

Folding the legs

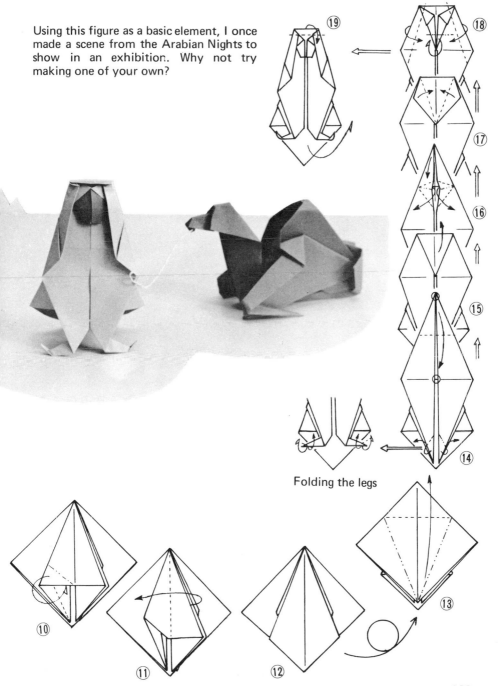

This Santa Claus is a compound figure made of four sheets of paper.

62. Santa Claus

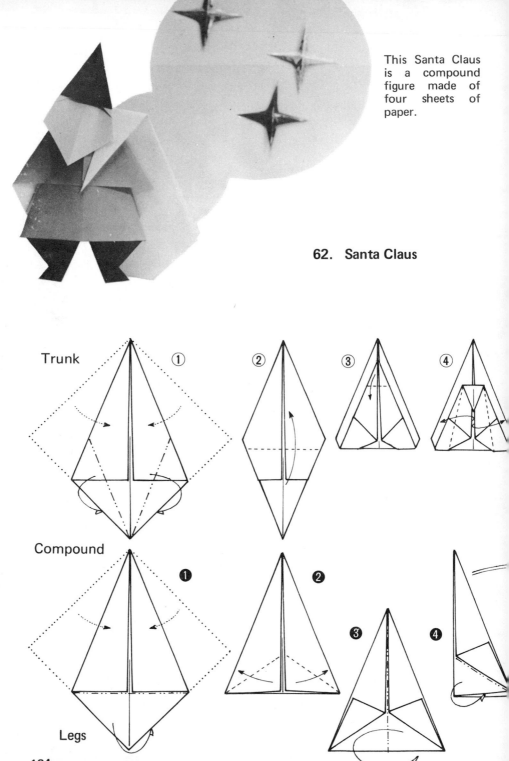

Trunk ① ② ③ ④

Compound ❶ ❷ ❸ ❹

Legs

The reindeer are compounds of two sheets of paper each.

⑤

⑥

⑦

❺

⑧

⑨

⑩

Origami Ideas for Future Study

Origami is a game that one plays with paper. There are people who call it an art. I suppose that this is a reflection of the natural desire to obtain recognition and a high evaluation for the things that a person find's interesting. I share this desire, but I prefer to call origami a game because there can be no more magnificent amusement than one that enables me to use my hands in such a way that from my fingertips birds fly, flowers bloom, and human figures come to life. Because of the nature of this game, the general tendency is to regard origami works as realistic representational things. So far, no book or other full treatment of abstract origami has appeared. But like other fields of endeavor, origami can certainly have main streams and branch currents, one of which can be abstract figures. As this field has yet been little explored, I present a few abstract origami here in the hope that they will inspire you to devote attention to what is likely to become a promising line of origami thought. The abstract origami have no names, but they are, I think, lovely to look at. Please try making some of your own.

A Few Last Words

Let me express my gratitude to the reader who has persevered this far with *Origami Made Easy*. The book ends here, but I hope this will be only the beginning of your origami study. As I have said, the major pleasure of origami is developing ingenuity to create better figures. I have carefully selected the works shown in this book and feel that they are good. But there may be some that do not come up to your standards. If so, please start at once thinking of ways to improve them. In fact, stimulating a desire to study and improve origami is my main purpose. When you devise origami that are better than what you find here, share them with your family and friends and, if opportunity presents itself, with me. I am convinced that through sharing both the study and the pleasure of origami, people in many lands can develop friendships that will, in their way, contribute to the peace of the world. It is true that among origami specialists are many people who pride themselves on their own achievements. But this is not necessarily bad. In fact, if such pride leads to friendly rivalry, nothing good be better.

Born in a distant age of peace, origami has been carefully nurtured over many centuries. It is my hope that we can continue to develop it and pass it on to other generations into the distant future.